With motivational words from Navigator founders to current leaders, this "must read" collection reminds me of Matthew 13:52 (MSG): "Then you see how every student well-trained in God's kingdom is like the owner of a general store who can put his hands on anything you need, old or new, exactly when you need it."

LINDY BLACK, associate US director, The Navigators

I cannot recommend these "Essential Writings of Knowing Christ and Making Him Known" strongly enough. I have read and utilized each of the articles herein many, many times over my forty-plus years of making disciples. They have been favorite "go to" tools of mine for years. What's new, then? Just the fact that they will be all together in one place! What a fantastic initiative. God wants to use your life—all your days. I'm absolutely sure of that. I'm also persuaded that these historic articles will help you greatly in that pursuit. I commend them to you wholeheartedly, even as I thank God for this sacred path you are on.

TOM BOURKE, national cities strategy, The Navigators

LIFE CHANGE LIBRARY

Essential Writings on Knowing Christ
and Making Him Known

A NavPress resource published in alliance
with Tyndale House Publishers

NavPress

NavPress is the publishing ministry of The Navigators, an international Christian organization and leader in personal spiritual development. NavPress is committed to helping people grow spiritually and enjoy lives of meaning and hope through personal and group resources that are biblically rooted, culturally relevant, and highly practical.

For more information, visit NavPress.com.

Life Change Library: Essential Writings on Knowing Christ and Making Him Known

Copyright © 2021 by The Navigators. All rights reserved.

Expanded from NavClassics © 2008 by The Navigators

A NavPress resource published in alliance with Tyndale House Publishers

NAVPRESS and the NavPress logo are registered trademarks of NavPress, The Navigators, Colorado Springs, CO. *TYNDALE* is a registered trademark of Tyndale House Ministries. Absence of ® in connection with marks of NavPress or other parties does not indicate an absence of registration of those marks.

The Team:
David Zimmerman, Acquisitions Editor; Elizabeth Schroll, Copy Editor; Olivia Eldredge, Operations Manager; Ron C. Kaufmann, Designer

Cover illustration of floral pattern copyright © Chantall/Depositphotos. All rights reserved.

Some of the anecdotal illustrations in this book are true to life and are included with the permission of the persons involved. All other illustrations are composites of real situations, and any resemblance to people living or dead is purely coincidental.

For information about special discounts for bulk purchases, please contact Tyndale House Publishers at csresponse@tyndale.com, or call 1-855-277-9400.

ISBN 978-1-64158-345-9

Printed in the United States of America

27	26	25	24	23	22	21
7	6	5	4	3	2	1

Navigators
Wayne Meyer
Oct 2022

CONTENTS

FOREWORD

THE LIFE OF A BELIEVER BEGINS with a seed. Big things often grow from small beginnings.

The beginnings of our salvation are mirrored in the process of a seed. In John 12:24 (NIV), Jesus says: "I tell you the truth, unless a kernel of wheat falls to the ground and dies, it remains only a single seed. But if it dies, it produces many seeds."

As followers of Jesus, we are the product of Jesus' death and resurrection. You and I are seeds that grow and mature in Christ through the nurturing power of the Holy Spirit (Mark 4:27; 1 Corinthians 3:6). And with faith as small as a mustard seed, a believer can walk in grace, power, and authority (Matthew 13:31-32).

The thing that's interesting to me about seeds is that they are both products and producers. Similarly, we are *products* of the grace of God, recipients of salvation. But we are also equipped by the Holy Spirit to be *producers* for the Kingdom of God, ambassadors of grace to a world in desperate need. As seeds, we become part of a reproductive legacy: spiritual generations.

We can trace this plan of reproduction all the way back to Abraham, who is told by God, "In thy seed shall all the nations of the earth be blessed" (Genesis 22:18). Paul tells us that Jesus is that seed of blessing (Galatians 3:16; read more on this in Doug Sparks's "Claiming the Promise" essay).

The metaphor of the seed can be traced throughout Scripture, and it reveals our two-part function as disciples of Jesus: We are meant to grow, and we are meant to multiply, just as seeds do.

The first function of a seed is to *know Christ*, to grow into him. Colossians 2:7 exhorts us to "Let your roots grow down into him, and let your lives be built on him. Then your faith will grow strong in the truth you were taught, and you will overflow with thankfulness" (NLT). You are I are invited to grow in the knowledge of Christ.

But our knowledge of Christ is not just for our personal satisfaction. The Great Commission's imperative to "Go and make disciples of all nations" is a call to *make Christ known* (Matthew 28:16-20, NIV). A seed is intended to sow new generations of believers, to participate in God's plan for reaching the nations.

Since its founding in 1933, The Navigators has committed to the mission "To know Christ, make Him known, and help others do the same." Our ministry has centered on the call to make spiritual generations of disciples and disciplemakers. If a disciple is a seed that grows, a disciplemaker is a seed that sows. In our vision for disciplemaking, we trust God to make us eager participants in the spiritual harvest.

This collection of life-changing essays highlights core

principles, not only to The Navigators' ministry, but to the life of every believer. Written by disciplemaking pioneers and spiritual parents, this resource energizes our vision and empowers our practice as lifelong disciplemakers.

Disciplemakers are not just sowers of good seed; we are benefactors of good seed that has been sown in us! Contributors to this resource have been leaders and influencers through Navigator history. As the current U.S. President of The Navigators, I stand on their shoulders and have personally benefited from their thinking. While the disciplemaking movement we are building on today can be traced back to people like The Navigators' founder, Dawson Trotman, most of the work of the Great Commission occurs through everyday people in every walk of life.

As you read this compilation, consider that you and I are the living harvest of small-seed investments planted long ago. Perhaps it was a Bible study leader who discipled you, a family member who introduced you to Jesus, or a printed resource like this one that pastored you into deeper knowledge of Christ. Regardless of the pathway, you and I are disciples because of disciplemakers.

For this reason, the potential of a seed cannot be overstated. My prayer for you is that you would continue to grow in Christ and become a multiplying force for His Kingdom. May you know Him and make Him known, all for the glory of God.

Doug Nuenke
U.S. President of The Navigators

KNOWING CHRIST

1

MARKS OF A DISCIPLE

Lorne C. Sanny

Lorne Sanny became president of The Navigators in 1956 after the death of Dawson Trotman. Sanny previously led the Navigator ministry in Seattle and served as vice president of The Navigators under Trotman. He spent many years working closely with Billy Graham, directing counselor training and follow-up for Graham's worldwide crusades. After stepping down from his role as Navigator president in 1986, Sanny went on to launch The Navigators' Business and Professional Ministry and serve as a speaker and mentor to Navigator staff around the world. He died March 28, 2005. Marks of a Disciple *was originally published in 1975.*

"AND JESUS CAME AND spake unto them, saying, All power is given unto me in heaven and in earth. Go ye therefore, and teach all nations, baptizing them in the name of the Father, and of the Son, and of the Holy Ghost: Teaching them to observe all things whatsoever I have commanded you: and, lo, I am with you alway, even unto the end of the world" (Matthew 28:18-20).

"Go ye therefore, and teach all nations." Another translation (NASB) puts it, "Go, therefore, and make disciples of all the nations."

Jesus came to this earth to be an example. He came here to show us the Father. He came here to take our sins in His own body on the cross, and He came to destroy the works of the Devil. And while He went about His ministry, along the way He also gathered up people to follow Him. They were called disciples.

Jesus was popular: "And there went great multitudes with him" (Luke 14:25). Yet he told them, "If any man come to me, and hate not his father, and mother, and wife, and children, and brethen, and sisters, yea, and his own life also, he cannot be my disciple. And whosoever doth not bear his cross, and come after me, cannot be my disciple" (Luke 14:26-27). He also said, "So likewise, whosoever he be of you that forsaketh not all that he hath, he cannot be my disciple" (Luke 14:33).

He turned to the crowds that were following Him and three times said to them, "cannot be my disciple . . . cannot be my disciple . . . cannot be my disciple." It's as if He said, "I am not looking for crowds; I'm looking for disciples."

Columnist Walter Lippmann once said, "There are only two kinds of people in the world that really count today, and they are the dedicated Christians and the dedicated communists." And *Time* magazine reported that the French communist Roger Garaudy feels that there are only two major forces in the world today—communism and Christianity.

And I know that among the Christians, the ones who really count are the disciples. As a friend of mine, a Christian leader, said, "Lorne, you don't find many disciples. But when you find one, there's almost no limit to what God can do through him."

How do you recognize a disciple? What does he look like?

What are his characteristics? Are you a disciple? Am I a disciple? I have studied seven or eight passages in the Scriptures having to do with the characteristics of a disciple. They can conveniently be boiled down to three marks of discipleship. When you see these three, you have a disciple.

Identified with Christ

The first mark of a disciple is that he is someone who is identified with the person of Jesus Christ—someone who will openly admit that he belongs to Christ. Now whatever else you may think about baptism, it is a public identification with Jesus Christ. When you are baptized, you are saying, "I take my stand with, I am on the side of, I belong to Jesus Christ."

A friend of mine told me of a Jewish man he led to Christ in Dallas. A few weeks later my friend told another Jewish man, a non-Christian, about the first one. Immediately the second man asked, "Has he been baptized yet?" When my friend said, "No, he hasn't," he replied, "Well, he'll never last." It was later, when the first Jew was baptized, that his family cut him off. He had made open identification with Jesus Christ.

"If thou shalt confess with thy mouth the Lord Jesus, and shalt believe in thine heart that God hath raised him from the dead, thou shalt be saved. For with the heart man believeth unto righteousness; and with the mouth confession is made unto salvation" (Romans 10:9-10). An open identification with Jesus Christ. Jesus promised, "Whosoever therefore shall confess me before men, him will I confess also before my Father which is in heaven" (Matthew 10:32).

A friend told me that when he went with Billy Graham, who was to speak to five hundred men at the Jewish Rotary Club of New York City, he wondered what in the world Mr. Graham would speak on to a Jewish club. When the time came, Billy stood up and spoke on "Christ: The Fulfillment of the Old Testament Prophecies." At the close they gave him a standing ovation. He had identified himself unashamedly with Jesus Christ.

On one occasion Jesus asked the disciples, "Who do you say that I am?" Peter answered, "You are the Christ" (Mark 8:29, NASB). It seems everything in His ministry led up to this.

But the thing that strikes me is that *then* "He began to teach them, that the Son of man must suffer many things, and be rejected of the elders, and of the chief priests, and scribes, and be killed, and after three days rise again" (Mark 8:31). A little later He called the multitude and His disciples to Him and said, "Whosoever will come after me, let him deny himself, and take up his cross, and follow me. . . . Whosoever therefore shall be ashamed of me and of my words in this adulterous and sinful generation; of him also shall the Son of man be ashamed, when he cometh in the glory of his Father with the holy angels" (Mark 8:34, 38).

Some years ago when I was with the Billy Graham team in a crusade, a businessman came forward one night and received Christ. The following Sunday night he went to a church that he sometimes attended. After the service he walked up to one of the leading elders in this church and told him, "I was at the Billy Graham meeting last week out at the ballpark. I went forward and received Christ."

"I heard about it, and I am delighted," the elder replied.

Then the businessman asked the elder, "How long have you and I been associated in business?"

"About twenty-three years, I think."

"Have you known Christ as your Savior all those years?" the man asked the elder.

"Yes, I have," he answered.

"Well, I don't remember you ever speaking to me about Christ during those years," the man said. The elder hung his head, and the man continued, "I have thought highly of you. In fact, I thought so highly of you that I felt if anyone could be as fine a man as you and not be a Christian, then I didn't have to be a Christian either."

This elder had lived a good life before his friend, but he had not taken the added step of openly identifying with the One who enabled him to live that kind of life. Here was a fine man, but he did not have this first mark of a disciple of Jesus Christ.

When Jesus asks you to deny yourself, take up your cross daily, and follow Him, what do you think it means? Whatever else it means, I think it means to be identified with Christ, not only when it's popular but when it's unpopular. Not only when it's the thing to do but when it seems as if it's not the thing to do. I like the way the New English Bible puts Revelation 1:9.

John writes, "I was on the island called Patmos because I had preached God's Word and borne my testimony to Jesus."

I once talked to the chief of police of Stockholm, who was a Christian, and discovered he had been a delegate to Panmunjom back when the Korean truce was first signed. He had interviewed some of the Chinese soldiers as to whether they wanted to be repatriated. He told me about a soldier who came through one day and gave his testimony to the interrogators concerning his faith in Jesus Christ. There in the Red Chinese army was a disciple.

A friend of mine traveling by train from Finland to Moscow tried to smuggle in three suitcases full of Bibles. But the Russian colonel at the border took rather unkindly to this idea. In fact, he was a little upset. My friend Jack asked him, "Well, what are you so worried about? Why do you get so upset about someone bringing a Bible into your country?"

"It's a fairy story, nothing but fairy tales," the colonel replied.

"Don't you have fairy-story books in Russia?" Jack asked.

"Oh, yes."

"Well, what's the matter with another one?"

"Ay," said the colonel, "if they believe that Bible, then they won't believe in communism."

So after warning him not to preach and scaring him a little bit, Jack says they let him go on his way.

A few hours later a couple of conductors came by and began to engage Jack and his friends in conversation and to sell them on the merits of communism. It wasn't long before Jack couldn't stand it any longer. He began to preach back to them. After he'd preached to them for a little while, one of the conductors pointed to another conductor at the other end of the car and said, "Now, he's one of yours. That conductor, he's one of your kind."

Later Jack talked to this conductor. Sure enough, he was a born-again Christian. They asked him if he had a Bible. He replied, "No, the last Bible in our town was owned by my grandmother. She tore it up into segments and distributed it to Christians around the town so it couldn't be confiscated all at once."

They asked if he'd like a Bible. (The colonel had confiscated only two of the suitcases of Bibles they had with them.) When they handed him a Bible, he wept and kissed it. Then he wrapped it in newspaper to take it off the train so it wouldn't be taken away from him.

I believe the striking thing about this story is that not only was there a Christian conductor on that train, but the other conductors knew he was a Christian. There was a disciple, identifying himself with the person of Jesus Christ.

Do you take an opportunity to admit that you are a follower of Jesus Christ? Why not determine that at the first opportunity this week you will quietly, graciously, but openly identify yourself with Jesus Christ? This is a mark of a disciple.

One morning I spoke to the SWAP (Salesmen with a Purpose) Club in Colorado Springs. They call in various speakers to tell how selling applies to their business. I spoke on how it applies to the gospel. In the process I explained the gospel.

After I had spoken, they introduced the guests. One of them was a friend of mine, Will Perkins, a Plymouth dealer. It was his first time there. When he was introduced, he stood and said, "Gentlemen, two years ago I heard a presentation similar to the one you heard this noon. I bought it, and it has changed my life." Then he sat down. I wondered how many Christians would have taken that little opportunity to identify themselves with the person of Jesus Christ.

Obedient to the Word

A disciple is not only a believer who is visibly identified with the person of Christ, he is also obedient to the Word of Christ— to the Scriptures. "Go therefore and make disciples of all the nations . . . teaching them to observe all that I commanded you."

"Teaching them to observe all that I commanded you." Jesus said, "If ye continue in my word, then are ye my disciples indeed" (John 8:31). If you observe it and apply it to your life, then you are His disciple.

Luke records what happened one day when a crowd of people listened to the Lord Jesus preach. One woman in the crowd was probably middle-aged or a little beyond (I'm interpreting a little bit here). As she listened to Jesus, something welled up within her. Perhaps she had a son who was wayward, and as she looked at the Lord Jesus, she wished her son were like Him. Or maybe she had never had a son and had always wanted to have one. Anyway, she spoke up—she sort of burst out—and said, "Blessed is the womb that bare thee" (Luke 11:27).

Jesus' answer to her was significant. He said, "Yea rather, blessed are they [or happy are they] that hear the word of God, and keep it" (Luke 11:28). That's real blessedness, real happiness—to hear what God has to say and to do it.

I enjoyed reading a book by the late Sam Shoemaker, *Extraordinary Living for Ordinary Men.* In it he says that Christians who are half-committed are half-happy. But to be really happy you need to go all the way in commitment. And this means to be obedient to the Word of Christ.

Obedience is necessary also for stability. The greatest sermon ever preached was the Sermon on the Mount. Notice how Jesus concluded it. He said, "Therefore whosoever heareth these sayings of mine, and doeth them, I will liken him unto a wise man, which built his house upon a rock: and the rain descended, and the floods came, and the winds blew, and beat upon that house; and it fell not: for it was founded upon a rock. And every one that heareth these sayings of mine, and doeth them not, shall be likened unto a foolish man, which built his house upon the sand: and the rain descended, and the floods came, and the winds blew, and beat upon that house; and it fell: and great was the fall of it" (Matthew 7:24-27).

What made the difference between the wise man and the foolish man? It wasn't knowledge, because they both heard the same sermon. They went to the same conference; they had the same knowledge. They both heard the Word. Not only that, they had the same circumstances. It says that the rain descended, the floods came, the winds blew and beat upon the house of the wise man. The rain descended, the floods came, the winds blew and beat upon the house of the foolish man. The circumstances were the same. One couldn't say, "Well, you don't know how tough it is where I come from." "Well, you don't know what kind of family life I've got." "You don't know how I suffer down at work." It wasn't their circumstances that made the difference. One thing made the difference between wisdom and foolishness: One obeyed the Word; the other one did not.

Jesus said, "He that hath my commandments, and keepeth them, he it is that loveth me: and he that loveth me shall be loved of my Father, and I will love him, and will manifest myself to him" (John 14:21). What does that mean? It means Jesus will make Himself real to him. To whom? To the one who has His Word and keeps it.

So a disciple does more than attend meetings. He does more than take notes. (He does that, incidentally, in my opinion, though I don't have any Scripture to prove it.) But he finds out what the Bible says and does it. Suppose he's going through Proverbs in his morning quiet time, and he comes to Proverbs 3:9-10, "Honour the LORD with thy substance, and with the firstfruits of all thine increase: So shall thy barns be filled with plenty, and thy presses shall burst out with new wine."

Early in my marriage, a Christian doctor in Seattle said, "Now let me make a suggestion about handling your family finances. Honor the Lord with your substance, and with the firstfruits of all your increase. Set aside money for the Lord before you pay the rent. Before you buy the food. Even when you think you don't have enough money left to pay the rent and to buy the food. You watch. God will see to it that you have money for the rent and for the food."

Now will He or won't He? Well, the Word promised that He would, and He did.

A friend of mine was looking over the family bills, and they looked pretty big. He and his wife prayed and decided that the first thing they ought to do to get out of debt was to increase their giving. And they are out of debt. They proved that God can fulfill His Word.

Another illustration of obedience to the Word of Christ is in these words of Jesus: "Therefore if thou bring thy gift to the altar, and there rememberest that thy brother hath ought against thee; leave there thy gift before the altar, and go thy way; first be reconciled to thy brother, and then come and offer thy gift" (Matthew 5:23-24).

When was the last time you went and made something right with someone else? When did you admit to your wife or your children that that fit of temper was sin? It's amazing to me when couples say that neither one has ever asked forgiveness of the other. If you don't find some times when you've got to make some things right, you're about ready for heaven right now. A disciple has a conscience void of offense toward God and man.

Let's go back to "Go therefore and make disciples of all the nations." I don't know why it is that some people think the day of missions is over. In one recent year, independent missions in America—not the denominational, just independent missions—needed four thousand missionary candidates that they didn't get.

Have you ever considered the possibility that obedience to the Word of Christ might mean leaving your business?

Bob Potter owned a supermarket in Oklahoma City. If he and his wife hadn't sold it and gone into the Lord's work, maybe God would have used someone else. But many people have been blessed by the ministry of Bob Potter through The Navigators.

Many times as I've gone around with the Billy Graham Crusades, young fellows have come up and said, "Mr. Sanny, do you know of any openings in Christian work?"

"Yep, I do."

They'd ask, "Where?"

And I'd say, "Right where you live. Your neighborhood. Where you go to school." I find that God usually leads you to the next step after you take this one. That's where you start.

I'm not speaking of going to the mission field because you're so sick and tired of the office you can't stand it, or because the boss has bugged you for two years and any change would be an improvement. I'm speaking of obedience to the Word of Christ, wherever it may lead and when the going is tough. That's a mark of a disciple.

After Moses died, Joshua had the job of taking three million people into the promised land. That included women, children, and livestock. God gave him some instructions. You'd think the Lord would say, "Now look, here's how you handle this problem, here's how you do this, here's how you do that." But, no. He said, "Joshua, one thing above all else is going to take a lot of courage—and it's not leading all these people and facing all the enemies that are in the land. That isn't what's going to take courage." Instead he said, "Only be thou strong and very courageous, that thou mayest observe to do according to all the law" (Joshua 1:7).

You may think it doesn't take courage to be obedient to the Word of God. But I wonder how obedient we really are to the Word. We live in a Christ-rejecting world, and anyone who is going to live in obedience to this Book is going to come into conflict with it. That's how you recognize a disciple. He does more than hear the Word. He puts into practice what he's heard.

The Navigators are kind of rabid on this subject. Year after year you'll hear us beat certain drums all the time. One is that we need to come to know the Bible and apply it. That's why we publish Bible study courses and Scripture-memory programs. We need to make up our minds that with God helping us and by the power of the Holy Spirit, we *are* going to be obedient to the Word of Christ. That's a mark of a disciple. He seeks to follow the Bible and do what it says.

Fruitful for Christ

So a disciple is one who is openly identified with the person of Christ. Second, he is obedient to the Word of Christ. And third, he is bearing fruit in the work of Christ. "My Father is glorified by this, that you bear much fruit, and so prove to be My disciples" (John 15:8, NASB).

Now it seems to me that there are two kinds of fruit here. First, the fruit of character, the fruit of the Spirit—"love, joy, peace, longsuffering, gentleness, goodness, faith, meekness, temperance" (Galatians 5:22-23). And second, there's fruit by way of influencing the lives of others for Christ. "Ye have not chosen me, but I have chosen you, and ordained you, that ye should go and bring forth fruit, and that your fruit should remain" (John 15:16).

I really threw a curve ball to my Sunday school class one Sunday morning. I intended to. We were talking about Jesus sending out the twelve two by two. He gave them authority over unclean spirits. They went out and preached that men should repent. They cast out demons and anointed with oil many who were sick and healed them. Then I asked, "Do you think Judas went out and preached to people to repent? Do you think Judas cast out demons and healed the sick?"

Some feel they can prove that Judas was never saved. Let's assume they're right. Did Judas then preach that people should repent? Did he cast out demons? Did he heal the sick? Could he have?

Look at Jesus' words: "Many will say to me in that day, Lord, Lord, have we not prophesied in thy name? and in thy name have cast out devils? and in thy name done many wonderful works? And then will I profess unto them, I never knew you: depart from me, ye that work iniquity" (Matthew 7:22-23).

My point was that we get so carried away with the spectacular that we think that is the supreme evidence that we are real disciples or Spirit-filled. But the real evidence is shown in our character—love, joy, peace, longsuffering, gentleness, goodness, faith, meekness, temperance. We're considering here the character of a disciple.

I've heard it said that the apostle Paul, before he was converted, would pray something like this every day, "God, I thank You that I am not a Gentile, that I am not a slave, and that I am not a woman." But look at how God changed his attitude. In his first letter he wrote, "There is neither Jew nor Greek, there is neither bond nor free, there is neither male nor female: for ye are all one in Christ Jesus" (Galatians 3:28). Here is evidence of the fruit of the Spirit in the way of character.

This is what it means to be a disciple of Jesus Christ. It includes one's whole attitude, outlook, character, and relationship to others. By this shall all men know that you are my disciples—if you can work great miracles? No. "By this shall all men know that ye are my disciples, if ye have love one to another" (John 13:35).

When Jesus talked about His ministry and what He came to do, He quoted from Isaiah 61:1, 3: "The Spirit of the Lord God is upon me; because the LORD hath anointed me to preach good tidings unto the meek; he hath sent me to bind up the brokenhearted, to proclaim liberty to the captives, and the opening of the prison to them that are bound . . . to give unto them beauty for ashes, the oil of joy for mourning, the garment of praise for the spirit of heaviness."

Take this world in which we live with all of its glitter, its tinsel, and its veneer. Strip all of this away, and how would you characterize the real world underneath? Brokenhearted, captive, bound, anxious, sad, depressed.

A disciple is one who gets involved in that kind of world, who is bearing fruit in the work of Christ. He shows the fruit of the Spirit in a Christlike character—love, joy, peace, long-suffering, gentleness, goodness, faith, meekness, temperance. How we need that in the world in which we live!

The Greatest Is Love

What did Jesus say was the greatest identifying mark of all in a disciple? Love. "By this shall all men know that ye are my disciples"—if you do what? "If ye have love one to another."

One of the greatest illustrations of this that I have seen was on the television special *James Emory Bond*. It was an entire one-hour interview with a black man who was an ex-truck driver. He was in his seventies at the time of the interview. Apparently he lived in Baltimore. One night he watched a panel discussion with some of the city leaders, mayor, chief of police, and others on television. They discussed the race and juvenile delinquency problems in Baltimore. As he watched, his heart was really moved.

The next day he went down to the television station. He wanted to talk to somebody because he had been so moved by their discussion. He said he knew the answer, but he didn't know whom to tell. At the station they had the good sense not only to interview him, but also to videotape it. All you saw was this gray-haired gentleman as he answered questions coming from off camera.

He said, among other things, that when he was a young fellow growing up on the edge of Baltimore, the white boys would throw rocks at him as he was on his way to school. He began to hate white people. As a young man he started working as a truck driver. One morning when he saw the milk truck go by, he thought how nice it would be if he could just have a little milk before he went to work in the morning.

He stopped the milkman, who was a white man, one day and asked him if he would leave him a quart of milk. He said, "No, I don't deliver milk to n*****s."

"So," he said, "the milk came, a quart each morning. Several weeks went by and I realized that he wasn't leaving me a bill, and I wanted to pay for it. So I stopped him one morning and said, 'I want you to give me a bill so I can pay for this.' And the milkman said, 'I don't take money from n*****s.' So I said, 'Well, I've got to pay you, you've just got to let me pay you.'

"'Well,' the milkman said, 'tell you what you do. You put the money on the fence post.'"

James Emory Bond said, "I thought I'd have a little fun with him, so I said, 'Now I won't feel like I paid you unless I put it in your hand.' 'No sir,' he said, 'put it on the post.' So I said, 'Okay.' And I put it on the post. When the milkman reached out to take the change, I just laid my hand on top of his. And he jerked it away."

Then he said, "Later on, one of God's servants by the name of Billy Sunday came to our town, and he told how Jesus Christ died on the cross to take away man's sin and his enmity of heart toward his fellow man. As I heard that, I realized that I needed this, and I walked the sawdust trail. And you know, God took the hate out of my heart for the white man. He put love there."

Apparently a few days later, unknown to him, the milkman also went to hear Billy Sunday. He went forward in the meeting, received Christ, and a couple days later pulled up in front of James Emory Bond's little place. With tears streaming down his face, he apologized for the way he had treated him. And this dear old black man said, "I have loved him, and he has loved me ever since."

Now that's what discipleship means. There is a mark of a disciple. Bearing fruit in the work of Christ. "By this shall all men know that ye are my disciples, if ye have love one to another." When we begin to see more disciples sprinkled around America and around the world, what a difference it will make! Real genuine disciples who will turn the world upside down. There are many already, and we ought to be praying for them.

But not only is there the fruit of Christlike character, but also the fruit of the Spirit in the lives of others. Jesus said, "Ye have not chosen me, but I have chosen you, and ordained you, that ye should go and bring forth fruit, and that your fruit should remain" (John 15:16).

Go and bring forth fruit. Paul wrote to the Romans of his desire: "That I might have some fruit among you also" (Romans 1:13). I think he meant lives influenced for Christ.

Once while I was thinking about this, two events took place that drove the truth home to me. One was something I read about Dr. Charles F. McKoy of Oyster Bay, Long Island. After fifty years of fruitful ministry as a pastor and evangelist, this seventy-one-year-old bachelor began looking around for a retirement home. A bishop from India came to his church to plead for missionary help for India. Dr. McKoy prayed earnestly that God might lay it on the heart of someone in the congregation to respond to this call and go to India. After the third message the bishop turned to Dr. McKoy and said, "I don't think God is looking for someone in the congregation. I think he is looking for the man in the pulpit."

Dr. McKoy could hardly believe his ears. He said, "Bishop, are you losing your mind? I'm seventy-one, I've never been overseas; I've never been on the ocean. The thought of flying terrifies me." But soon a new missionary was on his way to India, green and seasick, but on his way—at age seventy-one. Fifteen years later Dr. McKoy died. Between the ages of seventy-one and eighty-six he had gone around the world nine or ten times winning people to Christ in India and Hong Kong, in the opium dens and in the most difficult places. He was a real disciple in old age also. And I think one reason it struck me was that I was reading in Psalm 92:14, "They shall still bring forth fruit in old age; they shall be fat and flourishing." Your life can be fruitful to the very end.

The same week, we received word from Virginia that a young fellow named Teed Radin, twenty-three years of age and a graduate of Virginia Polytechnic Institute, who would soon be on the Navigator staff, had been in a head-on collision. Teed was killed instantly, and his fiancée died within the hour. One of the fellows wrote that while at Virginia Tech, Teed had led twenty-five to thirty men to Christ. Among them, five were dedicated, trained, effective men of the cross who, according to this person, would be willing at a moment's notice to die for the cause of Christ.

Dr. McKoy—an old man, a disciple to the end. Teed Radin—a young man, a disciple early in life. In fact, there's no better time to become a disciple than right now. But deep down in our hearts—that's where real business is done with God—we must determine that by God's grace and with the help of the Holy Spirit, we will be true followers of Jesus Christ.

Let's ask ourselves, *Am I a true disciple?*

Am I willing to be openly identified with the person of Jesus Christ?

Am I seeking to be obedient to the Word of Christ in my everyday life?

Am I bearing fruit in the work of Christ—by way of Christlike character and by influencing the lives of others?

I want to be a disciple. I want to have these marks and characteristics in my life. The only thing I'd like to do beyond that is to help make disciples and to get them to help make others. That's what Jesus wants done. *"Go therefore and make disciples of all nations."*

2

HOW TO SPEND
A DAY IN PRAYER

Lorne C. Sanny

How to Spend a Day in Prayer *was originally published in 1962.*

Avail yourself of the greatest privilege this side of heaven. Jesus Christ died to make this communion and communication with the Father possible.

BILLY GRAHAM

Prayer is a powerful thing, for God has bound and tied himself thereunto.

MARTIN LUTHER

God's acquaintance is not made hurriedly. He does not bestow His gifts on the casual or hasty comer and goer. To be much alone with God is the secret of knowing Him and of influence with Him.

E. M. BOUNDS

"I NEVER THOUGHT A DAY could make such a difference," a friend said to me. "My relationship to everyone seems improved."

"Why don't I do it more often?"

Comments like these come from those who set aside a personal day of prayer.

With so many activities—important ones—clamoring for

our time, real prayer is considered more a luxury than a necessity. How much more so spending a *day* in prayer!

The Bible gives us three time-guides for personal prayer. There is the command to "pray without ceasing"—the spirit of prayer—keeping so in tune with God that we can lift our hearts in request or praise anytime through the day.

There is also the practice of a quiet time or morning watch—seen in the life of David (Psalm 5:3), of Daniel (Daniel 6:10), and of the Lord Jesus (Mark 1:35). This daily time specified for meditation in the Word of God and prayer is indispensable to the growing, healthy Christian.

Then there are examples in the Scripture of extended time given to prayer alone. Jesus spent whole nights praying. Nehemiah prayed "certain days" upon hearing of the plight of Jerusalem (Nehemiah 1:4; 13:6). Three times Moses spent forty days and forty nights alone with God (Exodus 24:18; 32:20-31; 34:28).

Learning from God

I believe it was in these special times of prayer that God "made known his ways" and His plans to Moses (Psalm 103:7). He allowed Moses to look through a chink in the fence and gain special insights, while the rank-and-file Israelites saw only the *acts* of God as they unfolded day by day.

Once I remarked to Dawson Trotman, founder of The Navigators, "You impress me as one who feels he is a man of destiny, one destined to be used of God."

"I don't think that's the case," he replied, "but I know this.

God *has* given me some promises that I know He will fulfill." During earlier years, Daws spent countless protracted time alone with God, and out of these times the Navigator work grew—not by methods or principles but by promises given to him from the Word.

In my own life, one of the most refreshing and stabilizing factors, as well as the means for new direction or confirmation of the will of God, has been those extended times of prayer—in the neighborhood park in Seattle, on a hill behind the Navigator home in Southern California, or out in the Garden of the Gods here in Colorado Springs.

These special prayer times can become anchor points in your life, times when you "drive a stake" as a landmark and go on from there. Your daily quiet time is more effective as you pray into day-by-day reality some of the things the Lord speaks to your heart in protracted times of prayer. The quiet time, in turn, is the foundation for "praying without ceasing," going through the day in communion with God.

Perhaps you haven't spent a protracted time in prayer because you haven't recognized the need for it. Or maybe you aren't sure what you would do with a whole day on your hands *just to pray.*

Why a Day of Prayer?
Why take this time from a busy life? What is it for?

1. For extended fellowship with God—beyond your morning devotions. It means just plain being with and thinking about

God. God has "called [us] unto the fellowship of His Son Jesus Christ" (1 Corinthians 1:9). Like many personal relationships, this fellowship is nurtured by spending time together. God takes special note of times when His people reverence Him and *think upon His Name* (Malachi 3:16).

2. For a renewed perspective. Like flying over the battlefield in a reconnaissance plane, a day of prayer gives opportunity to think of the world from God's point of view. Especially when going through some difficulty, we need this perspective to sharpen our vision of the unseen and to let the immediate, tangible things drop into proper place. Our spiritual defenses are strengthened while "we fix our eyes not on what is seen, but on what is unseen. For . . . what is unseen is eternal" (2 Corinthians 4:18, NIV).

3. For catching up on intercession. There are non-Christian friends and relatives to bring before the Lord, missionaries on various fields, our pastors, neighbors, and Christian associates, our government leaders—to name a few. Influencing people and changing events through prayer is well-known among Christians but too little practiced. And as times become more serious around us, we need to reconsider the value of personal prayer, both to accomplish and to deter.

4. For prayerful consideration of our own lives before the Lord—personal inventory and evaluation. You will especially want to take a day of prayer when facing important decisions, as well as on a periodic basis. On such a day you can evaluate where you are in relation to your goals and get direction from the Lord through His Word. Promises are there for you and me, just as they have been for Hudson Taylor or George Müller or Dawson Trotman. And it is in our times alone with God that He gives inner assurance of His promises to us.

5. *For adequate preparation.* Nehemiah, after spending "certain days" seeking the Lord in prayer, was called in before the king. "Then the king said unto me, For what dost thou make request? So I prayed to the God of heaven. And I said unto the king, If it please the king . . ."—and he outlined his plan (Nehemiah 2:4-5). Then Nehemiah says, "I arose in the night, I and some few men with me; neither told I any man what my God had put in my heart to do at Jerusalem" (Nehemiah 2:12). When did God put in Nehemiah's heart this plan? I believe it was when he fasted and prayed and waited on God. Then when the day came for action, he was ready.

I heard a boy ask a pilot if it took quick thinking to land his plane when something went wrong. The pilot answered that no, he knew at all times where he would put down *if* something went wrong. He had that thought out ahead of time.

So it should be in our Christian life. If God has given us plans and purposes in those times alone, we will be ready when opportunity comes to move right into it. We won't have to say, "I'm not prepared." The reason many Christians are dead to opportunities is not because they are not mentally alert, but they are simply unprepared in heart. Preparation is made when we get alone with God.

Pray on the Basis of God's Word

Daniel said, "In the first year of [Darius's] reign, I, Daniel, understood from the Scriptures, according to the word of the LORD given to Jeremiah the prophet, that the desolation of Jerusalem would last seventy years. So I turned to the Lord God and pleaded with him in prayer and petition, in fasting, and in sackcloth and ashes. I prayed to the LORD my God and confessed" (Daniel 9:2-4, NIV).

He understood by the Scriptures what was to come. And as a result of his exposure to the Word of God, he prayed. It has been said that God purposes, therefore He promises. And we can add, "Therefore, I pray the promises, so that God's purposes might come to reality." God purposed to do something, and He promised it; therefore, Daniel prayed. This was Daniel's part in completing the circuit, like an electrical circuit, so that the power could flow through.

Your day alone with the Lord isn't a matter of sitting out on a rock like a statue of *The Thinker* and taking whatever thoughts come to your mind. That's not safe. It should be a day exposed to God's Word, and then His Word leads you into prayer. You will end the day worse than you started if all you do is engage in introspection, thinking of yourself and your own problems. It isn't your estimate of yourself that counts anyway. It's God's estimate. And He will reveal His estimate to you by the Holy Spirit through His Word, the open Bible. And then the Word leads into prayer.

How to Go about It

How do you go about it? Having set aside a day or portion of a day for prayer, pack a lunch and start out. Find a place where you can be alone, away from distractions. This may be a wooded area near home or your backyard. An outdoor spot is excellent if you can find it, but don't get sidetracked into nature studies and fritter away your time. If you find yourself watching the squirrels or the ants, direct your observation by reading Psalm 104 and meditating on the power of God in creation.

Take along a Bible, a notebook and pencil, a hymnbook, and perhaps a devotional book. I like to have with me the booklet *Power Through Prayer* by E. M. Bounds and read a chapter or two as a challenge to the strategic value of prayer. Or I sometimes take Horatius Bonar's *Words to Winners of Souls*, or a missionary biography like *Behind the Ranges*, which records the prayer victories of J. O. Fraser in inland China.

Even if you have all day, you will want to use it profitably. So lose no time in starting, and start purposefully.

Wait on the Lord

Divide the day into three parts: waiting on the Lord, prayer for others, and prayer for yourself.

As you *wait on the Lord*, don't hurry. You will miss the point if you look for some mystical or ecstatic experience. Just seek the Lord, waiting on Him. Isaiah 40:31 promises that those who wait upon the Lord will renew their strength. Psalm 27:14

is one of dozens of verses that mention waiting on *Him*, as is Psalm 62:5 (NIV)—"Find rest, O my soul, in God alone; my hope comes from him."

Wait on Him first *to realize His presence*. Read through a passage like Psalm 139, grasping the truth of His presence with you as you read each verse. Ponder the impossibility of being anywhere in the universe where He is not. Often we are like Jacob when he said, "Surely the LORD is in this place; and I knew it not" (Genesis 28:16).

Wait on Him also *for cleansing*. The last two verses of Psalm 139 lead you into this. Ask God to search your heart as these verses suggest. When we search our own hearts, it can lead to imaginations, morbid introspection, or anything the enemy may want to throw before us. But when the Holy Spirit searches, He will bring to your attention that which should be confessed and cleansed. Psalms 32 and 51, David's songs of confession, will help you. Stand upon the firm ground of 1 John 1:9 and claim God's faithfulness to forgive whatever specific thing you confess.

If you realize you've sinned against a brother, make a note of it so you won't forget to set it right. Otherwise, the rest of the day will be hindered. God won't be speaking to you if there is something between you and someone else that you haven't planned to take care of at the earliest possible moment.

As you wait on God, ask for the power of concentration. Bring yourself back from daydreaming.

Next, wait on God *to worship Him*. Psalms 103, 111, and 145 are wonderful portions to follow as you praise the Lord for the greatness of His power. Most of the psalms are prayers. Or turn to Revelation chapters 4 and 5, and use them in your praise to Him. There is no better way to pray scripturally than to pray Scripture.

If you brought a hymnbook, you can sing to the Lord. Some wonderful hymns have been written that put into words what we could scarcely express ourselves. Maybe you don't sing very well—then be sure you're out of earshot of someone else and "make a joyful noise unto the LORD" (Psalm 100:1). *He* will appreciate it.

This will lead you naturally into thanksgiving. Reflect upon the wonderful things God has done for you and thank Him for these—for your own salvation and spiritual blessings, for your family, friends, and opportunities. Go beyond that which you thank the Lord for daily, and take time to express appreciation to Him for countless things He's given.

Prayer for Others
Now is the time for the unhurried, more detailed prayer for others whom you don't get to ordinarily. Remember people in addition to those for whom you usually pray. Trace your way around the world, praying for people by countries.

Here are three suggestions for what to pray:

First, ask specific things for them. Perhaps you remember or have jotted down various needs people have mentioned. Use requests from missionary prayer letters. Pray for spiritual strength, courage, physical stamina, mental alertness, and so on. Imagine yourself in the situations where these people are and pray accordingly.

Second, look up some of the prayers in Scripture. Pray what Paul prayed for other people in the first chapter of Philippians and Colossians, and in the first and third chapters of Ephesians. This will help you advance in your prayer from the stage of "Lord, bless so and so and help them to do such and such."

Third, ask for others what you are praying for yourself. Desire for them what the Lord has shown *you*.

If you pray a certain verse or promise of Scripture for a person, you may want to put the reference by his name on your prayer list. Use this verse as you pray for that person the next time. Then use it for thanksgiving as you see the Lord answer.

Prayer for Yourself

The third part of your day will be prayer for yourself. If you are facing an important decision, you may want to put this before prayer for others.

Again, let your prayer be ordered by Scripture, and ask the Lord for understanding according to Psalm 119:18. Meditate upon verses of Scripture you have memorized or promises you have previously claimed from the Word. Reading a whole book of the Bible through, perhaps aloud, is a good idea. Consider how it might apply to your life.

In prayer for yourself, 1 Chronicles 4:10 (NIV) is one good

example to follow. Jabez prayed, "Oh, that you would bless me and enlarge my territory! Let your hand be with me, and keep me from harm so that I will be free from pain." That's prayer for your personal life, your growth, God's presence, and God's protection. Jabez prayed in the will of God, and God granted his request.

"Lord, what do *You* think of my life?" is the attitude of this portion of your day of prayer. Consider your main objectives in the light of what you know to be God's will for you. Jesus said, "My food . . . is to do the will of him who sent me and to finish his work" (John 4:34, NIV). Do you want to do God's will more than anything else? Is it really your highest desire?

Then consider your activities—what you *do*—in the context of your objectives. God may speak to you about rearranging your schedule, cutting out certain activities that are good but not best, or some things that are entanglements or impediments to progress. Strip them off. You may be convicted about how you spend your evenings or Saturdays, when you could use the time to advantage and still get the recreation you need.

As you pray, record your thoughts on your activities and use of time, and plan for better scheduling. Perhaps the need for better preparation for your Sunday school class or personal visit with an individual will come to your mind. Or the Lord may impress on you to do something special for someone. Make a note of it.

During this part of your day, bring up any problems or decisions you are facing and seek the mind of God on them. It helps to list the factors involved in these decisions or problems. Pray over these factors and look into the Scriptures for guidance. You may be led to a promise or direction from the passages with which you have already filled your mind during the day.

After prayer, you may reach some definite conclusions upon which you can base firm convictions. It should be your aim in a day of prayer to come away with some conclusions and specific direction—some stakes driven. However, do not be discouraged if this is not the case. It may not be God's time for a conclusive answer to your problem. And you may discover that your real need was not to know the next step but to have a new revelation of God Himself.

In looking for promises to claim, there's no need to thumb through looking for new or startling ones. Just start with the promises you already know. If you have been through the Topical Memory System, start by meditating on the verses in the "Rely on God's Resources" section. Chew over some old familiar promises the Lord has given you before, ones you remember as you think back. Pray about applying these verses to your life.

I have found some of the greatest blessings from a new realization of promises I already knew. And the familiar promises may lead you to others. The Bible is full of them.

You may want to mark or underline in your Bible the promises the Lord gives during these protracted times alone. Put the date and a word or two in the margin beside them.

Variety is important during your day of prayer. Read awhile, pray awhile, then walk around. A friend of mine paces the floor of his room for his prayer time. Rather than get cramped in one position, take a walk and stretch; get some variety.

As outside things pop into your mind, simply incorporate those items into prayer. If it's some business item you must not forget, jot it down. Have you noticed how many things come to mind while you are sitting in church? It will be natural for things to occur to you during your prayer day that you should have done, so put them down, pray about them, and plan how you can take care of them and when. Don't just push them aside or they will plague you the rest of the day.

At the end of the day summarize in your notebook some things God has spoken to you about. This will be profitable to refer to later.

Two Questions

The result of your day of prayer should be answers to the two questions Paul asked the Lord on the Damascus road (Acts 22:6-10, NASB). Paul's first question was, "Who are You, Lord?" The Lord replied, "I am Jesus." You will be seeking to know Him, to find out who He is. The second question Paul asked was, "What shall I do, Lord?" The Lord answered him specifically. This should be answered or reconfirmed for you in that part of the day when you unhurriedly seek His will for you.

Don't think you must end the day with some new discovery or extraordinary experience. Wait on God and expose yourself to His Word. Looking for a new experience or insight you can share with someone when you get back will get you offtrack. True, you may gain some new insight, but often this can just take your attention from the real business. The test of such a day is not how exhilarated we are when the day is over but how it works into life tomorrow. If we have really exposed ourselves to the Word and come into contact with God, it will affect our daily life. And that is what we want.

Days of prayer don't just happen. Besides the attempts of our enemy Satan to keep us from praying, the world around us has plenty to offer to fill our time. So we have to *make* time. Plan ahead—the first of every other month, or once a quarter.

God bless you as you do this—and do it soon! You too will probably ask yourself, "Why not more often?"

3

CLAIMING THE PROMISE

Doug Sparks

Doug Sparks's service with The Navigators began in the mid-1950s, when Dawson Trotman sent him to Taiwan. He remained on staff for the next forty-five years, pioneering Navigator ministries throughout Asia, Europe, and the Middle East. He was still actively involved in missions at the time of his death in December 2003. Claiming the Promise *was originally published in 1991. Ralph D. Winter of the United States Center for World Mission called this essay a "remarkable" consideration of "the very backbone of the Bible"—the relationship between God's covenant with Abraham and the Great Commission.*

MY WIFE, LEILA, AND I HAD just returned from five exhausting but fruitful years in Taiwan. We were looking forward to rest— a time alone together away from the rush of ministry, a time of spiritual and marital renewal. Most of all we were looking forward to the birth of our first child, whom we were calling "the tiny world traveler." He was conceived in Taiwan and "traveled" through Southeast Asia, India, the Middle East, Europe, and back to the United States before his birth.

We were finally settled in beautiful Colorado Springs. Each day was marked by the exhilarating anticipation of becoming a family together!

Excitement was also in the air at The Navigators international headquarters, where a missionary team was being formed to minister among the Mau Mau terrorists in British detention centers. The Mau Mau had terrorized the countryside of Kenya, torturing and murdering fellow Kenyans who would not take the Mau Mau oaths and help them overthrow the British colonials. The rebellion had been broken, and the Mau Mau were rounded up and imprisoned by the tens of thousands. The church council of Kenya had invited The Navigators to preach and start Bible studies in the prison camps.

As I prayed about this I sensed that God was asking me to go with the team. Yet I protested in my heart. Leila was expecting; I wanted and needed to be at her side and share the miracle of birth with her. I wanted to be the first to behold our baby—to hold, to cuddle, to kiss him.

I shared the dilemma with Leila. We prayed; we surrendered. We asked God to let me stay, but we made ourselves available to Him and His perfect will.

We decided not to mention this to anyone but God, asking that, if it was His will, the Navigator leadership would ask me to join the Kenya team, and we could both know His peace in my going. And indeed, a few weeks later I was invited to go to Africa. With His accompanying peace, both Leila and I began making the necessary preparations. It was a tearful departure at the airport. What a surrendered, courageous, loving wife God had given me!

Our missionary team flew to London and the next day to

Nairobi, Kenya. The continent of Africa was before us. The Mau Mau terrorists provided our beachhead—a cruel, degenerate, murderous lot whom God loved, whom He wanted to forgive and transform into the beauty of Jesus.

What a response we witnessed to the gospel of Jesus Christ! In the first few weeks, hundreds responded to the Savior, who gave them life and hope where before there was emptiness and despair.

While in Africa, about a week before Leila was due to have our baby, I went out for a long walk and talk with God. I prayed over every detail I could imagine concerning the birth of our child, not knowing that at that very moment our son, Kent, was being born!

The prayer time felt inspired—God speaking things into existence through human lips. From praying for Leila and the baby, God led me to pray for Africa. The sky was filled with sparkling stars, shining brightly in a jet-black sky. They seemed to light up the earth. It was these stars shining in the darkness that reminded me as I prayed of God's promise to Abraham in Genesis 22:17-18:

> Indeed I will greatly bless you, and I will greatly
> multiply your seed as the stars of the heavens and as
> the sand, which is on the seashore; and your seed shall
> possess the gate of their enemies. And in your seed all
> the nations of the earth shall be blessed, because you
> have obeyed My voice (NASB).

As I was reviewing this promise in my mind, I began claiming it in prayer: "Oh, Lord, give us African disciples of Christ who will shine as lights throughout this dark continent. May they bless every tribe with the knowledge of Christ. May they conquer and possess the strongholds of Satan until the peoples of Africa experience the blessing of God."

God is true to His promise, and He is answering that prayer. Through the ministry of many Navigator missionaries and Africans, God is raising up disciples all over Africa who are blessed and multiplying.

So often we focus our prayers merely on ourselves and our circle of experience. We are like spiritual shut-ins in a world in which God is actually doing great and mighty things to fulfill His promise. We tend to stand on the sidelines, asking God for peanuts when we could be asking for continents.

The purpose of this essay is to demonstrate how to claim the promise of God in prayer. To effectively claim the promise, we should understand the answers to each of the following questions:

1. What is the meaning of the promise?
2. To whom is the promise given?
3. How does the promise work?
4. Who is the God of the promise?
5. How certain is the promise?
6. What is the need for the promise?
7. How do we claim the promise?

What Is the Meaning of the Promise?

In Genesis 12:1-3 (NIV) we read, "The LORD had said to Abram, 'Leave your country, your people and your father's household and go to the land I will show you. I will make you into a great nation and I will bless you; I will make your name great, and you will be a blessing. I will bless those who bless you, and whoever curses you I will curse; and all peoples on earth will be blessed through you.'"

It is encouraging to our faith to see that God *has* fulfilled a large part of His promise to Abraham. From Abraham *has* come a great nation and a great name—he is the father of all believers (Romans 4:11). The nation of Israel *did* possess the land and under kings David and Solomon became a mighty empire. Today, God is fulfilling the universal promise made to Abraham to bless all the peoples of the world through Christ.

John R. Stott, British theologian, Bible expositor, and author, said, "God made a promise to Abraham. And an understanding of that promise is indispensable to an understanding of the Bible and of the Christian mission. . . . The whole of God's purpose is encapsulated here."[1]

The blessing in this promise is salvation in all of its ramifications for every people on earth. Our common English use for the word *blessing*, "to confer well-being, happiness, or prosperity on," is totally inadequate and degrading if applied to this Scripture.

The word *blessing* here means "divine favor" in its ultimate sense. According to Dr. Ralph Winter, founder and director of the U.S. Center for World Mission, it means to "reinherit." To be blessed of God in this passage is to become a child of God with all its privileges and responsibilities. It is reinheriting that lost position of sonship. It is becoming a joint heir with Christ. It is also being involved in and committed to the family business—to bless all peoples of the earth.

The apostle Paul gives us the New Testament commentary on this promise in Romans 4 and Galatians 3. He expounds on the blessing: It is righteousness by faith, right-standing with a holy God, without works. It is the blessedness of complete forgiveness. It is justification through faith for everyone who believes in Jesus Christ. It is being indwelt by the Holy Spirit and receiving the divine nature. Christ in us becomes our hope of glory. The Spirit recreates us with the nature and presence of Christ in our lives.

To Whom Is the Promise Given?
God wants all of His children involved in His plan for the whole world through the promise to Abraham.

Are we as Christians presumptuous in claiming this promise? No. The promise is for all believers. It is our privilege and right to claim it in prayer for ourselves and for all the peoples on earth.

Notice how the New Testament affirms this: "So then, those who have faith are blessed along with Abraham, the man of faith" (Galatians 3:9, EHV); "If you belong to Christ, then you are Abraham's seed, and heirs according to the promise" (Galatians 3:29, NIV); and "Now you, brothers, like Isaac, are children of promise" (Galatians 4:28, ESV).

We are children and heirs who can claim the blessing of Abraham in prayer and by faith.

John Stott said, "Who then are the true descendants of Abraham, the true beneficiaries of God's promises to him? Paul does not leave us in any doubt. They are the believers in Christ of whatever race."[2]

God is no respecter of persons. He loves each one infinitely, tenderly, and compassionately. He delights to bless each people, each believer. It is His nature to do so. He is the Father and originator of loving-kindness, graciousness, mercy, and generosity. He is the very essence of "I will bless you."

The Father's purpose is not just to bless you but to extend the blessing through you to the peoples of the earth. The other side of the coin in blessing is sharing. After the promise "I will bless you" comes the divine imperative "You shall be a blessing" (Genesis 12:2, NASB).

In God's creation, He generates seed-bearing plants, fish, birds, animals, humans—all with their own unique seed to reproduce after their kind. God commands them in Genesis 1 to be fruitful and multiply and fill the earth.

God's plan in re-creation is similar. In Genesis 22:18 God tells Abraham, "In thy seed shall all the nations of the earth be blessed." Paul points out that this *seed* is Jesus Christ (Galatians 3:16).

So each believer is carrying about the seed of Jesus Christ to reproduce in another. God promises, "I will greatly bless you. I will greatly multiply you."

After rising from the dead, Jesus gathered His disciples and opened their minds to the Scriptures. They saw how He fulfilled the promises and the prophecies (Luke 24:44-47). Jesus then commanded His disciples to be His witnesses "to the uttermost parts of the earth" (Acts 1:8, WEB). In the Great Commission He commands, "Go and make disciples of all nations" (Matthew 28:19, NIV). What He commands, He enables us to do. He promised His presence and His power to disciple among all peoples. Having fulfilled the promise Himself, He is able to command us to fulfill it with His power.

Ralph Winter marries the promise of Genesis 12 with the Great Commission: "There is formidable scholarship that understands the mandate of Genesis 12:1-3, 26:4-5, and 28:14-15 as the first appearance of the Great Commission, pointing, as these verses do, to all the nations of the world, to a spiritual 'blessing' involving sonship, and to a mechanism consisting of human intermediaries. Thus, these are the foundation verses linking the whole Bible to the redemptive work of Jesus Christ and His mission to the nations."[3]

How Does the Promise Work?

The promise is claimed by faith. The Great Commission is obeyed by faith. The apostle Paul described the underlying principle: "Therefore, the promise comes by faith, so that it may be by grace and may be guaranteed to all Abraham's offspring" (Romans 4:16, NIV). *The operating principle of the promise is faith, that it may be by grace.*

Abraham believed God, and it was credited to him as righteousness. This came *before* circumcision, *before* the Law was given.

But some would say, "Didn't Abraham's obedience prompt God's fullest blessing?"

Yes, Abraham left his country and his household, but he didn't go out by his own works but by faith, responding in obedience, according to Hebrews 11. Later, when God commanded Abraham to offer his son Isaac as a sacrifice, we see that the motivation and power for obedience came from faith. "By faith Abraham, when God tested him, offered Isaac as a sacrifice" (Hebrews 11:17, NIV). Obedience was the result, the demonstration, of Abraham's faith. The condition of the promise is a live faith that *responds* in obedience.

Believing is actually responding to the faith God gives. It accepts righteousness as a gift, and therefore is not consumed with weighing our works to see if we are good enough for God to fulfill His promise to us.

One of the great problems within evangelical Christianity is that we receive the promise of Christ's blessing and salvation by faith, then lapse into trying to propagate this promise by our own works and worthiness. The world task before us requires far more than human effort. It requires a miraculous working of God in fulfillment of His impossible promise!

The key question we have to ask ourselves is, "What principle are we going to operate on in claiming this promise?" The principle of works? In other words, if I will do this, God will do that? The characteristic here is obligation. The result is that I get the credit. I can boast; I can find fulfillment in myself, in what I do. But I can never be sure I have done enough.

Or, are we going to operate on the basis of faith by grace? This focuses on what God says *He* will do, because He is gracious and fully able. I simply act accordingly. I step out in faith, believing God will do what He says. The result is that God gets the credit, and I find my fulfillment in God and what He has done according to His promise.

Somewhere along the way, each believer must make a choice. Will it be works or grace through faith? Which principle are you choosing? It is impossible for these contrary principles to coexist. Paul pointed this out: "And if [it be] by grace, then it is no longer by works; if it were, grace would no longer be grace" (Romans 11:6, NIV).

This indelible lesson was brought home to me when I was working in Europe. One day a young, newly married friend came into my office in London. She was in tears. Repeatedly she had gone to the embassy to get a visa so she could join her missionary husband in Africa, but the official was very rude to her and didn't want to be bothered.

We decided to pray together on the basis of Christ's worthiness and just because of His grace. When my friend returned to the embassy that same day, the same official cordially granted her visa. He even offered to call the airport for her!

It is *by His grace* that we have boldness and access to God to receive help for every need. We are confident, free, and motivated, then, to do the work of prayer—both for ourselves and for the unreached peoples of the world.

Never mind that we find our faith small compared to Abraham's. The criterion is not the strength of our faith but the focus of it. For our faith to grow we must grow in the knowledge of the object of our faith—God Himself.

Who Is the God of the Promise?

In the promise of Genesis 12:1-3, expressed either directly or indirectly, God the Father says seven times, "I will." Who is this God who says, "I will"?

To Abram God reveals Himself as El Shaddai, the God who says "I will" in Genesis 17:1-2. At this point, Abram was ninety-nine years old. According to Scripture, Sarai's womb was dead. It was physically impossible for Abram and Sarai to have a son. But it is when we humans are hopeless that we can best see who the God of promise really is and what He can do for us. *El Shaddai* means the Lord almighty, the Lord all sufficient, the God of infinite power and supply.

The object of our faith and prayer is God. What we ask

for—how we pray—is determined by our concept of who He is. To pray in truth, we must know the promise. To pray in power, we must know the God of promise.

Paul gives us some rich insights into the implications of El Shaddai in Romans 4:17—"the God who gives life to the dead and calls things that are not as though they were" (NIV). And in verses 18-21 we see Abraham's response in faith to that revelation of God:

> Against all hope, Abraham in hope believed . . . just
> as it had been said to him. . . . He faced the fact that
> his body was as good as dead. . . . Yet he did not waver
> through unbelief regarding the promise of God, but
> was strengthened in his faith and gave glory to God,
> being fully persuaded that God [El Shaddai] had
> power to do what he had promised.

Imagine an old man of ninety-nine having his name changed from Abram, meaning "exalted one" (which certainly described him), to Abraham, "the father of a multitude" and "the father of many nations"![4] His friends must have thought he had gone senile! But from Abraham's point of view, God had said it and Abraham was ready to "go public" with it. Abraham believed that God *had* made him a father of many nations. And, because he knew the One who had made the promise, he gave glory to God as though it were already true.

We need to see God as El Shaddai—the Lord almighty, the

Lord sufficient, the God of infinite power and supply who hears and answers prayer. This is the nature of the Promiser.

How Certain Is the Promise?

In claiming the promise, we must be utterly convinced of its certainty. God has said it. Christ has fulfilled it by becoming a man, dying to purchase our salvation, and rising again. Now He sits at the right hand of God to see the promise become a reality among the peoples of the earth. The promise is fulfilled already in the heavens. We need only to pray it down to earth.

The certainty of the promise is based on the integrity and power of the One giving it. God's promise in Genesis 12 was enough, but for our sakes He confirmed it with an oath in Genesis 22:16 to clarify its certainty: "By Myself I have sworn, declares the LORD" (NASB). The promise had already been given. It was true. God didn't have to give it again to make it true. He didn't have to use an oath to bind Himself to it. But the writer of Hebrews told us, "Because God wanted to make the unchanging nature of his purpose very clear to the heirs of what was promised, he confirmed it with an oath" (Hebrews 6:17, NIV).

An oath is like a contract. When you sign a contract, you are taking an oath that you will do certain things. This is a long-standing, universal practice. God gave this oath (and He could swear by no greater One than Himself) to let *us* know He meant it.

In the book of Revelation, we see a multitude that no man can number, from all the tribes and peoples and kindreds and tongues. They are standing before the throne of God, worshipping Him and praising Him. His kingdom *has* come; the promise is sure. In God's sight it is already done.

The key to certainty, then, is to ask God for what He has already said He wants to do! R. A. Torrey, internationally known preacher and author, has written, "Here is one of the greatest secrets of prevailing prayer: to study the Word to find what God's will is as revealed there in the promises, and then simply take these promises and spread them out before God in prayer with the absolutely unwavering expectation that He will do what He has promised in His Word."[5]

Now we know with certainty that it is the Father's will to bless or reinstate us and the peoples of all the earth as His heirs through Christ, so we may ask for it with confidence.

What Is the Need for the Promise?

God's love for those who have never heard is unfailing. He sees and cares about the peoples of the world, their temporal needs, their poverty, hunger, injustice, and suffering. He is deeply compassionate and desires to help them right now, where they are. He also sees beyond the temporal into the eternal. His love is an everlasting love, and He desires that each person on earth be in His family and kingdom now and forever.

God's approach to the peoples of the world is not a Band-Aid approach. It involves all the means of a holy, just, and loving God forgiving and justifying those who have both willfully and blindly gone their own way. He wants to transform them into Christlikeness and to make them all they were created to be. And so God gives a promise for such a blessing and through Christ provides the means to fulfilling the promise. He gives us, in turn, the command to act on it:

"Go . . . and preach the gospel to every creature"
   (Mark 16:15).
"Go and make disciples of all nations"
   (Matthew 28:19, NIV).

God's promise announces His *purpose* to bless all peoples of the world. Christ's Great Commission announces God's *program* for doing that today.

Over half of the 6.6 billion people who occupy our planet today live in Asia.[6] China is the first country with a population of over a billion people. Some estimate that by the year 2000 India will have a billion people.[7] But more formidable than the numbers are the thousands of ethnic languages and cultures that separate these peoples from each other and from the gospel.

Politically, 85 percent of Asians (2.3 billion) live in nations where missionaries are banned. Christians can enter these nations only as business and professional people, sharing their lives and witnessing for Christ on a personal basis. Christian ministries are suppressed. The vast majority of the peoples of Asia have never clearly heard the gospel of Jesus Christ.

We don't have the ability to reach the masses, to penetrate these cultures, languages, and deeply rooted ideologies. We don't have the army of disciplers to send to them. We don't have the power to overcome Satan's influence over these peoples. The task of evangelizing Asia is simply impossible for men.

Jesus said, "What is impossible with men is possible with God" (Luke 18:27, NIV). The One who made the promise to bless all the peoples of the earth is the One who has the power to do it. God's promise and God's power are working today in remarkable ways through God's people to accomplish this task. Today Christianity worldwide is growing at a rate of seventy thousand people daily.[8]

When the communists took over China in 1949, about three million claimed to be Christians. Today, conservative estimates indicate there are forty to fifty million Christians in China![9] Africa, too, has seen a phenomenal turning to Christ. Estimates are that by the year 2000 there will be 350 million African Christians—in only 120 years of missionary effort.[10]

God is on the move. He is implementing His plan for the earth. We must look to Him and the power of His promise to reach the remaining peoples of every tongue and tribe and nation who have yet to hear of Jesus Christ and the salvation He freely offers.

This missionary task can only be accomplished as we do these things:

> Believe the promise of God.
> Pray over the promise.
> Act on the promise.

How Do We Claim the Promise?

Seeing, then, that the promise is so certain and so needed, how can we be partakers of it? Our part in the promise to bless the nations is directly proportionate to our *faith* and our *prayers*.

What petitions should we bring to God? How should we pray the promise into being?

In Our Personal Lives

The Lord promises to bless us. We need to pray, "Lord, El Shaddai, You say You will pour forth Your life into me. I want to claim Your love in all my relationships. Pour forth Your love. When I'm tempted, pour forth Your holiness. When I'm anxious, pour forth Your peace. When there is injustice, pour forth Your justice. In my business dealings, pour forth Your integrity. When I'm wrong, pour forth Your mercy. When I'm disappointed and discouraged or depressed, pour forth Your joy."

When we pray and claim "I will bless you," we remember that we inherit this blessing because God is our Father and Christ's nature is alive in us by the power of the Holy Spirit. We believe it, ask it, expect it, act on it. We have the promise. We should pray in the manner of Ephesians 3:20, "Now to Him who is able to do exceedingly abundantly above all that we ask or think, according to the power that works in us" (NKJV).

In Our Direct Personal Relationships

The Lord promises, "You will be a blessing." When Christ becomes a reality in our lives, it will affect our relationships. His life will pour over and bless other people. God calls that multiplying! "I will *greatly* multiply you." "I will *surely* multiply you" (Genesis 12:2; 22:17, ESV, emphasis added).

In order to multiply, we have to let people into our lives to see the difference Christ makes—not a pseudodifference, not a way to act, but reality. They need to see Christ incarnated in us. That incarnation presses us into acting on their behalf. As we build bridges of mutual love, respect, and trust, the gospel message we declare will ring true.

I don't believe I would have ever come to Christ through talk, argument, or preaching. Over a period of months, I saw the tremendous change and blessing Christ made in an old high school buddy of mine. His faith was real, his love for me genuine. That is what made me want Christ's blessing, too, and I received Him into my life.

In fulfillment of the promise, the divine life is so poured into our lives by El Shaddai that it overflows and blesses others.

For the World

The Lord promises, "All peoples will be blessed through you." Our praying for the peoples of the world should reflect both the size of the promise and the greatness of the Promiser. The world is small, but God is big. He invites us, "Call to Me, and I will answer you, and show you great and mighty things, which you do not know" (Jeremiah 33:3, NKJV).

In praying for the peoples of the world, we wrestle with the powers of darkness. Satan is called "the ruler of this world," and he has far too long possessed and ruled over these peoples.

The powers of Satan must be defeated in prayer, and laborers with the good news of Jesus Christ must go to these people. This is why Jesus said, "The harvest is plentiful but the workers are few. Ask [beseech] the Lord of the harvest, therefore, to send out workers into his harvest field" (Matthew 9:37-38, NIV).

S. D. Gordon, theologian and prolific writer of the early twentieth century, said, "The greatest thing each one of us can do is to pray. If we go personally to some distant land, still we have gone to only one place. Prayer puts us into direct dynamic touch with the world. A man may go aside today and shut the door and as really spend a half hour of his life in India [or Lebanon or China] as though he were there in person. Surely you and I must get more half hours for this secret service."[11]

Many years ago, there was a very dedicated young Christian girl in the eastern United States. She was of poor health and could not be very active for the Lord, so she took upon herself a ministry of prayer. She became burdened for a little-known African Pygmy tribe and "adopted" them as her prayer target. She wrote many missionaries in the region to find out more about this tribe. The tribe was nomadic, constantly roaming to new areas. They were very difficult to reach and evangelize, but she claimed them as "her people."

She prayed faithfully day after day, week after week, year after year. Eventually her health worsened, and she died.

Twenty years later, Gospel Recordings, a specialized mission agency, rediscovered this tribe. Using interpreters, their missionaries recorded the gospel in the language of the tribe. Hundreds of records were made and played to this tribe. The response was extraordinary. These nomadic people heard the good news in their own language, the Holy Spirit worked, and they were wonderfully converted.

The degree of commitment and faith in this tribe was so unusual that Gospel Recordings decided to do some research. What had brought about such a response? Certainly it wasn't just the recordings.

When they discovered how this sickly young girl had prayed in faith for so many years, they concluded this had to be the reason. Her prayers had advanced the gospel among this tribe twenty years after her death. In God's time the answer had come down to earth. She had prayed from what was on God's heart, and He had brought it into being.[12]

When we pray, some answers come immediately. Others require waiting on our part, especially when we are praying for ourselves or the unreached peoples of the world. Changed lives require time—that is the way God works.

Jesus taught His disciples the importance of perseverance in Luke 18:1 (NIV): "That they should always pray and not give up."

Adoniram Judson was a man who prayed and persevered and labored in Burma. He went to Burma in 1824 at twenty-four years of age. He prayed day after day for God to change the course of that nation. He vowed he would not leave until the cross was planted there forever.

He persisted in prayer. After seven years one man became a disciple. After ten years Judson was mistreated, tortured, and imprisoned. His wife and child died. After sixteen years he had baptized more than one hundred converts. His second wife died, more children died, he nearly died. He continued to give much time to prayer. After forty years he died in Burma. At his death there were 63 churches, 163 missionaries and workers, and more than 7,000 converts in Burma. Judson had planted the cross in Burma forever. He claimed God's promise.[13]

Do you have this promise of God? Yes, you assuredly have it. Whether you neglect it or not, it is yours. Every believer has this promise.

But that's not the question to ask. The more pertinent question is, "Does the promise have you?" When the promise possesses you, Christ possesses you, and you will go anywhere, you will do anything, you will sacrifice, you will endure suffering, you will even die if necessary to spread the blessing to the peoples of the earth—and you will persevere in prayer to that end.

The promise possessed Christ. It drove Him to the cross. His last words before dying were "It is finished." He had fulfilled the promise. His last words on earth before He ascended were "But you will receive power when the Holy Spirit comes on you; and you will be my witnesses in Jerusalem, and in all Judea and Samaria, and to the ends of the earth" (Acts 1:8, NIV). The promise possessed Him, and by the power of the Holy Spirit it would possess the apostles and Christians following them until they witnessed to the salvation of Christ to all peoples—to the ends of the earth.

You can be part of that mighty succession and plant the cross forever among people—like Adoniram Judson or the young girl who prayed and prayed for the Pygmy tribe. She didn't go anywhere, but her prayers did, and for all eternity she can rejoice before God with the people she prayed into His kingdom.

Through believing and persevering prayer, you can have a significant part in multiplying the joint heirs with Christ among the peoples of the earth. That is the challenge of Christ's Great Commission. As someone has put it—"This is not the Great *Suggestion*." It is the last and most demanding mandate from our Savior King—that we go and make disciples among all peoples.

Whatever you decide to do with your life from here on, be sure it includes claiming the promise of God—which puts you into the world-blessing business. It is yours to experience personally and to use in extending God's kingdom globally. Those who are claimed by the promise claim the promise more effectively.

For Reflection and Action

You can start right now to claim God's promise in prayer!

1. With what one specific characteristic of Christ (His mercy, love, courage, etc.) would you like God to strengthen you? Ask God to strengthen you with this characteristic so that you can be a blessing to the people in your local world.

2. What blessing from the life of Christ is already a strength in your life? How could you apply this blessing to influence someone else this week? Talk with God about this.

3. Ask God which of the peoples of the world you could begin praying for this week. For whom would He like you to start claiming His promise? How can you start finding out about some nation in the world so that you can pray with wisdom?

4. Finally, ask the Lord to write His promise on your heart until it grips you.

4

CHANGING YOUR
THOUGHT PATTERNS

George Sanchez

George Sanchez was on staff with The Navigators for four decades. Prior to that he served with missionary radio station HCJB in Quito, Ecuador. Before retiring from The Navigators, he served as a counselor and teacher presenting seminars and conferences around the world. After moving to Albuquerque, New Mexico, George ministered to businessmen and couples seeking to reach the unchurched. He currently lives in a retirement facility, where he continues to seek the Lord. He originally gave this message in 1977 as part of a series on interpersonal relationships.

"I wish I could stop being impatient with my children!"

"What can I do to keep from feeling guilty and depressed?"

"How can I have victory over my negative imagination?"

As I counsel with people, questions and statements like these are constantly mentioned. What they are asking basically is, "How can I change? How can I bring my thoughts under control and develop new attitudes?"

Change—Who Needs It?
Experiences we have had, including those in childhood, make impressions on us. These experiences cause us to respond in

certain ways to situations we face later in life. This is a common pattern for all of us. One person never experienced an outward manifestation of affection from his father, and now he struggles with a deep need for that kind of expression. Another was made to feel he could never do anything properly, so today he battles with a sense of uncertainty and inferiority. Another was deeply hurt by someone to whom he reached out, and now he finds it difficult to trust anyone. But there are also the positive experiences. Many people experienced love, acceptance, support, and encouragement as children. They are able, as life develops, to relate more easily to people and circumstances.

Where the patterns are negative and destructive, the person needs change so he can find release and experience a new freedom—freedom that comes from knowing the truth and how to apply it. "Then you will know the truth, and the truth will set you free" (John 8:32, NIV). Where the patterns have been positive and affirming, they can be developed and reinforced by utilization and specific, planned action.

The important fact to recognize is that our thought patterns and habits *can be changed* constructively, and we can experience release from reactions and responses that continually defeat us.

Hope for Change
Let's look at a typical pattern of thinking. First, we recognize that there is a need to change an attitude, whatever that attitude

may be. Maybe it's an attitude toward an individual or situation. In order to change his attitude, the Christian resorts to prayer. He hopes his attitude will change as a result.

We have been instructed that the way to change is through the means of prayer. After we pray, somehow something is supposed to happen and our attitudes change. We may not say it that way, but there is the implication that some mystical process takes place and attitudes change when a person reads the Bible or prays.

We recognize that there is a certain truth to that concept. The Bible says it, so we know that there has to be truth in it. "How can a young man keep his way pure? By living according to your word" (Psalm 119:9, NIV). God is the only One who can bring about real change in our thought patterns. We must always keep that in mind.

However, people repeatedly struggle in vain for results in this pattern—they pray and ask for help but nothing happens. No change of attitude takes place. They continue to struggle with the same basic conflicts. When this happens, a pattern of defeat begins.

Of course, the enemy takes advantage at this point and begins accusing, "You see, there must be something else wrong, or this attitude would change." So people look deeper, pray harder, spend longer periods of time with the Lord, and still many of these attitudes don't change. This is a real issue which we are going to encounter continually in our relationships with people.

Basis for Change

In considering this, we want to be very careful to avoid any idea of a "do-it-yourself" Christianity. We do not make the changes in our lives. Only *God* has the power to make deep inner changes. I want to emphasize that so there is no misunderstanding.

On the basis of Proverbs 4:23, "Watch over your heart with all diligence, For from it flow the springs of life" (NASB), and other Scripture, we encourage people to saturate their hearts—their minds basically—with the Word of God. We believe that the more saturation takes place, the more people's conduct and way of thinking are going to be affected. Again, this is a true concept. But to experience change, we must put into practice the truths with which we are saturating our minds.

Renewing the Mind

To begin to understand how this applies to the concept of changing our thought patterns, let's examine one little phrase from Paul, "Be transformed by the *renewing of your mind*" (Romans 12:2, NASB, emphasis added). Every one of us must seek to answer the all-important and practical question, "How do I renew my mind?"

Let's use a hilltop as an illustration. When rain falls on a hill, the water drains off. How does it drain off? In rivulets. Initially, they are just small rivulets, but each time rain falls, the rivulets cut deeper and deeper. They can become deep chasms.

Now let's compare these rivulets with thought patterns

in our minds. The longer we think along any given line, the stronger that thought pattern becomes. Every time we react in a certain way, we reinforce that thought pattern. This is how habits are formed.

If we want to get rid of rivulets on a hill, we could take a bulldozer and cover them up. We could also build a little dam where the rivulet begins so that the next time it rains the rivulets will change course. While we can't cover up our thoughts with a mental bulldozer, we can build a dam in our minds when certain thoughts begin. We can refuse to think them. We can say, "I will not allow myself to think that."

Redirecting Our Thoughts

Building a dam in the mind, however, is not enough. That is, saying "no" is not sufficient by itself. We also need to provide a new course for our thinking. We should not just suppress thoughts; we should redirect them. We should change negative thought patterns into positive thought patterns.

We find a good illustration of this in Paul's words: "He who has been stealing must steal no longer, but must work, doing something useful with his own hands, that he may have something to share with those in need" (Ephesians 4:28, NIV). How does a thief stop being a thief? Is it just by not stealing anymore? Not quite. Certainly that is part of it. That's saying "no" to a negative, destructive habit. It's building the "dam." But it's not enough. In order to change, the thief is told to get a job and earn money honestly. Then he is to give to others in need so that perhaps they won't be tempted to steal. *Now the process is complete.* The negative habit has been dealt with by an act of the will, which is choosing to stop it. But the will must also choose to replace that with the corresponding constructive action in order that the change in thought patterns may be complete.

And so it becomes clear that to change these thought patterns we must do two things. First, we must build the dam; that is, refuse to allow wrong thoughts. Second, we must redirect the flow and develop a new way of thinking. Eventually the old patterns will fade. They may never disappear, but they will fade and will become less and less influential in controlling our thinking.

We need to realize that this takes place by an act of the will, not by wishful thinking and not solely by devotional meditation and prayer. Meditation and prayer are necessary, but we must move beyond that to an act of the will.

"Put Off" and "Put On"

Paul gives us some helpful thoughts on the subject: "Set your minds on things above" (Colossians 3:2, NIV). This is a declarative statement that involves an act of the will. You set your mind. He continues, "Put to death . . . whatever belongs to your earthly nature: sexual immorality, impurity, lust, evil desires" (verse 5, NIV), "You must rid yourselves" (verse 8, NIV), and "put on" (verse 12, NASB). Changing thought patterns is not just "putting away" by building dams, but also "putting on" by building new patterns. It is not just suppressing but redirecting our thoughts into healthy, positive ways of thinking.

What does "put to death" (verse 5, NIV) mean? The old thought patterns do not just die naturally. It would be great if they did, and we never again had this desire or that temptation. But because "the heart is more deceitful . . . and is desperately sick" (Jeremiah 17:9, NASB) and lusts against the Spirit, these battles go on continually. Therefore, the statement "put to death" requires a continual action. We must put old thought patterns to death every time they rear their heads. We cannot just put immorality to death and then no longer have immoral thoughts. They will continue to come up, and every time they do, we have to stop them right at the headwaters with that dam. *Every time!* The more times we put those wrong thoughts to death and put on the new ones, the less our thoughts will tend to flow in the wrong direction.

Paul commands us to develop healthy, positive, spiritual ways of thinking (Colossians 3:12). We are to "put on" certain positive thought patterns as we "put off" the wrong ones. These two steps are essential if there is to be genuine change. We have looked at the illustrations of the changed thief (Ephesians 4:28). In the same passage Paul gives another helpful illustration of "putting off" and "putting on." He states that the liar is to stop (put off) lying but immediately reminds us that he must speak (put on) the truth (4:25). Not only does the liar stop lying, but he begins telling the truth. The two steps are clear—"put off" and "put on."

Crucified with Christ

Paul deals with this concept in his letter to the Romans (chapters 6–8). It helps to have some one-word titles for these passages. Romans 6 describes our *provision*. We have been delivered from the power of sin. "Our old self was crucified with him so that the body of sin might be done away with, that we should no longer be slaves to sin" (verse 6, NIV). "Because anyone who has died has been freed from sin" (verse 7, NIV). "Sin shall not be your master" (verse 14, NIV). "You have been set free from sin" (verse 18, NIV). *Provision* has been made so that we might overcome the power of sin.

Struggle is the key word in chapter 7. We struggle all the time. We struggle about how to get the provision of chapter 6 into our lives. The solution is the Lord Jesus Christ (verse 25). He is always the final answer. We all believe this. We preach sermons on it. We teach it. But too often we have not told people how to experience it in a practical way.

Chapter 8 gives us the *solution*. One phrase is repeated several times. Different versions state it in different ways, but the idea is the same. They all refer to "setting the mind." "Those who are in accord with the flesh *set their minds* on the things of the flesh, but those who are in accord with the Spirit, [*set their minds* on] the things of the Spirit. For the *mind set* on the flesh is death, but the *mind set* on the Spirit is life and peace, because the *mind set* on the flesh is hostile toward God" (verses 5-7, NASB, emphasis added).

Add to that these words of Paul, "Fix *your thoughts* on what is true and good and right. *Think about* things that are pure and lovely, and dwell on the fine, good things in others. *Think about* all you can praise God for and be glad about" (Philippians 4:8, TLB, emphasis added).

There, in essence, is the whole concept of what is commonly called the power of positive thinking: "Fix your thoughts." It is a statement of command which requires a response of the will—to fix our thoughts—to set our minds on these things.

The practical application of this concept is this: "Continue to work out your salvation with fear and trembling, for it is God who works in you to will and to act according to his good purpose" (Philippians 2:12-13, NIV). Note, it says "work out," not "work for," your salvation. We can compare this to a builder who has a set of plans that he must work out in order to do his job. In the same way we have been given "plans" regarding the Christian life that we are now responsible to "work out"; in other words, to put spiritual truth into action through obedience.

This verse presents the chronological process of the effective outworking of Romans 6–8. Another version states, "For God is the Energizer within you, so as to will and to work for His delight" (Philippians 2:12, MLB).

Our Responsibility

A light switch can be used to illustrate the Christian's responsibility in this process. As the light switch is moved, it turns the light on and off. That switch connects to a wire that goes through the house and out to a power line that eventually goes to a generating plant. Millions of volts of electricity are being produced there. The source of energy is enormous. The power comes through the lines to the wall switch. Whether the light is illuminated by the electrical energy depends on the position of the switch. The switch is a circuit breaker.

In the same way, what happens in the first part of Paul's statement determines whether the energy in the second part comes into our lives. Continually working out our salvation has to do with what we think—what we fix our thoughts on, what choices of will we make. In effect Paul says, "You do your part. You do what you know is right, then God will energize you to accomplish the right choice you make." This means we should renew our thoughts and not allow them to continue following negative patterns. Thus we are turning the "switch" on for God's energy to flow whenever we choose not to allow wrong thoughts to continue. This is difficult and requires personal discipline.

Ingrained Thought Patterns

Thought patterns are so ingrained that we don't recognize the stimulus that sets them off. And before we know it, one of our old thought patterns is off and running downhill. We respond to it as fast as a snap of the fingers. For example, when we hear the word "fireplace," we immediately see an image—good, bad, or indifferent. The words "ocean beach" immediately bring a specific picture to mind. These words are stimuli that induce an immediate thought pattern.

In the same way, there are many things that "trigger" or set off wrong thought patterns. We need to ask God to alert us through His Holy Spirit the minute these negative thought patterns begin.

That is all we can legitimately ask Him to do. When we ask God to change our thought patterns, we are asking Him to do something for which He has already said we are responsible.

Interpersonal Conflicts

Let's consider conflict in an interpersonal relationship as an illustration. One person says, "I have prayed for months, literally, for love for that person, but I just can't love him." However, when God says we are to do something, it is never a question of "can't" but "won't." God commands us to love others, whether or not they are our enemies, whether or not they have mistreated us. We are to love each other. No matter how we feel, God commands that we demonstrate the qualities of love (1 Corinthians 13:4-7) by an act of our will in obedience to that command. As we act in obedience, our feelings will respond accordingly. "A new command I give you: Love one another" (John 13:34, NIV). The issue is not "can't" but "won't."

There are many similar areas in which we often find ourselves asking God to change something when He has told us what to do. He tells us clearly that it is our responsibility to "*fix our thoughts*" and "*set our minds*." We have the right to ask God to alert us to the beginning of that negative thought pattern, but as soon as He alerts us, then the responsibility to take action is ours.

Example for Men

One of the areas that men have a great deal of difficulty with is their eyes—what they look at. We teach men that it is their responsibility to control their eyes. And while that emphasis may be proper, it presents a problem. The problem is that we are asking them to suppress a normal reaction. The Bible refers specifically to this. We are told in the words of the Lord Jesus that if a man looks on a woman to lust after her, he has committed adultery in his heart. Jesus didn't say it was wrong to look at a woman. He said it was wrong to look and lust. There is a difference.

Jesus never condemned seeing what normally crosses our line of sight, even when it's an attractive woman. Yet, we condemn it. We ask a man to act contrary to normal reaction, producing an immediate conflict. The moment a man looks at anything that might cause lust, he feels guilty. It is as though he shouldn't see or is supposed to wear blinders. It produces a tremendous amount of frustration.

What we should do is help men realize that looking at someone or something that is attractive is normal. However, how a man handles his subsequent thoughts is important. If he allows himself to dwell on lustful desires for that person or thing, according to Jesus, he is sinning. But I would emphasize that the same stimulus can be used to produce a positive response as well as a negative one.

Years ago when I began to realize this, I learned for the first time how to have real victory in this area of my own thought life. I remember how revealing and liberating it was. Whenever I would find myself looking at an attractive woman who could have generated wrong thoughts, I would admit them and control them by saying, "Thank You, Lord. Thank You that I am healthy, that I have normal responses, that I am made the way You intended me to be made, and thank You for a wonderful wife with whom I can enjoy what You have given me."

It only took a split second, but a dam was built and a new positive channel was constructed. It happened very quickly. By the grace of God, that has become a thought pattern now.

If I were a single man I would say the same thing, but the last phrase would read, "And thank You that in Your own time You will allow me the privilege of enjoying this part of my life, if that is Your plan for me." In either case, the principle is the same; that is, utilizing the same stimulus that could produce negative thoughts to produce positive responses instead by choosing that which I am going to allow my mind to think about.

I did not suppress those feelings. I did not say, "Come on, George, you are not supposed to think that way." That only reinforces the negative response I am trying to overcome.

Suppression reinforces negativism. Sublimation or redirection reinforces a positive replacement of that negative thought. So, the same stimuli can produce positive results if we are alert to catch them the moment our thoughts begin a negative pattern. We do this by building a "dam" by saying no to the destructive thought and yes to a positive, constructive alternative.

Building the Dams

This is where Scripture comes in. Verses or concepts of Scripture can be used to build these dams which check our thinking. The next time that same thing stimulates our thinking we shouldn't say, "Don't think that way," but instead we should tell ourselves, "Don't think that way; *think this way.*" This redirects those thought patterns into positive directions. "Fix your thoughts on what is true and good and right" (Philippians 4:8, TLB).

If we do what God requests (Philippians 2:12), then He promises to energize us (verse 13). We submit our wills to His. We decide by an act of the will not to continue in the old patterns but to let Him change us. He promises to do that. All we do is throw the switch by saying no to wrong thoughts and yes to the right ones. Then the energy from His enormous source of power flows through us and energizes us to do the very thing we want to do and that He wants us to do. Thus, it is not by our efforts that this is accomplished. *He produces the change, but we must make the choice.*

Dealing with Our Feelings

Let's look at another personal example. I found that in my relationship with my wife, Florine, I am not beyond feeling impatient. I never will be. As long as I am in this body and have the heart of flesh that I have, I am going to have these tendencies. But I find now that I am able to recognize these impatient feelings.

Speaking of feelings, I think it's important to understand a few things about them. It seems to me there is an emphasis that says, "Christians shouldn't have certain feelings." As a result, many sincere people find themselves struggling with guilt because they still have feelings they are told they shouldn't have. Feelings are normal to every human being. In themselves they are neither good nor bad. They simply are. We all experience them—anger, resentment, envy, jealousy, defensiveness, lust, and others. These are part of the temptations spoken of by Paul (1 Corinthians 10:13). The important thing is what we do with these feelings. A follower of Christ is not to be controlled by his feelings. This is what Proverbs 25:28 (NIV) refers to as self-control.

Well then, how do we handle these feelings? This triad should help answer that:

1. Our emotions respond. As we've seen, we all have feelings that are set off by a variety of stimuli. It's important that we admit these feelings. It is destructive to try to deny or suppress them. But, as followers of Christ, we must not be controlled by these initial reactions.

2. Our intellects (minds) evaluate. We are responsible to "set our minds" and think through our emotional responses and their possible results. It is at this point that the Bible is so important. The more we know of what the Bible says, the more truth we have by which to evaluate our reactions. This will also help us know what to do with the feelings we are experiencing.

3. Our wills choose. Having had the initial reaction and having evaluated, we now must choose our course of action. *Here is the crucial step!* Our evaluation may have told us that our feelings (reactions) are not biblical—they are neither constructive nor loving. In spite of this we may choose to act on the basis of feelings. This would be an immature response and behavior. It is also disobedience and sin (James 4:17). However, the mature choice, the one we have been discussing in order to change our thought patterns, is to heed the evaluation and act responsibly, even though our feelings might be otherwise.

One added word of caution. Sometimes after having submitted our will to God and disciplined ourselves to set our mind, we might become confused and fatigued when we don't experience the change we desire. In such cases, it is advisable to seek a mature, godly friend or biblical counselor to whom we can freely express our thoughts and feelings. There may be a need for other significant changes in our lifestyle, patterns of relationships, compulsive behavior, or confusion in equating desires with needs. Talking and praying with such a person helps clarify issues and guides us in making wise choices and changes, both in lifestyle and thought patterns.

Now back to my feelings of impatience. When I recognize them, I admit them to God, myself, and Florine, so that she might understand and even give me added support. Then, by an act of my will, I determine, with God's help, to demonstrate patience because that is what love is. "Love is patient, love is kind" (1 Corinthians 13:4, NASB). I have found that as quickly as I do that, God energizes me to be patient! I have been surprised to see the distinct change that takes place from one brief moment to another. It is not because of my ability, but because I choose to submit my will to God's will. As a result, God energizes me.

Jesus Christ, Our Sufficient Rescuer

Paul is right when he refers to Christ as the One "who will rescue me from this" (Romans 7:24, NIV). The Lord Jesus Christ is the One. But first we must be willing to change our thought patterns—we must set our minds, fix our thoughts on what is true and good and right, and submit our wills to His. In other words, we must do our part. Then God can release the energy that He wants to give us to accomplish His purpose.

5

GETTING TO KNOW
GOD THROUGH A DAILY
QUIET TIME

Mike Jordahl

Mike Jordahl and his wife, Nancy, live in Colorado Springs, where Mike currently serves as a Senior Vice President for The Navigators and leads National Staff Recruiting. Mike met Christ as a high school senior living in Madrid, Spain, and then was helped by Navigators at Illinois State University to grow as a Christ-follower and disciplemaker. Mike and Nancy have served on The Navigator staff since 1981 in Iowa, Kansas, Massachusetts, and now, Colorado. "Getting to Know God through a Daily Quiet Time" was first published in 2013.

OF ALL THE THINGS THAT HAVE helped me know God better, having a daily quiet time is at the top of the list. First as a college student, and then in my early twenties, when I was working as an office manager and then for a newspaper, I found that my intimacy with Christ was directly related to my daily quiet times. Now that I'm in my mid-fifties, having a daily quiet time continues to be a spiritual lifeline for me.

Throughout thirty years of working with college students and then, in recent years, with people in their twenties, I have taught thousands of young men and women—in large groups, small groups, and especially one-to-one—about how to cultivate their walk with God through having a daily quiet time.

I am excited now to share with you what I have learned about getting to know God through a few minutes of prayer and reading the Bible on a daily basis. For some, what I share here will be brand-new. If that is you, I am praying that the few words you are about to read will bring you both joy and depth in your relationship with God. For others, this will all be review. If that's the case, I pray that the reminders you find here will add new life to your relationship with Christ.

Not for Me . . .

The first time I heard the phrase "quiet time," I was a high school senior and a new follower of Christ. I recall overhearing some people who I thought were very committed to God using the phrase, and since I wanted to be committed, too, I thought I should try having a "quiet time."

A few days later, I found a spot where I could sit and be quiet, but that is all I knew: to be quiet. I realize now that sometimes just sitting in silence can be a very useful experience, but back then I just sat and wondered when "it" would happen. I wasn't sure what "it" was, but I imagined that something "spiritual" would surely happen if I just sat quietly.

Well, nothing happened that day. And nothing happened the next day either; so I decided that quiet times were not for me. After all, I had tried sitting quietly, but doing so had not made me feel especially spiritual.

My First Real Quiet Time

Fast-forward to my freshman year of college, when I met some believers in my residence hall who were involved in The Navigators. One of them, an upperclassman named Cary, asked me if I would like to have a quiet time with him the next day.

Hmmm, that's a little odd, I thought to myself. (I imagined myself just sitting quietly with another dude.) *Well, maybe that's the trick to the whole quiet time thing,* I reasoned. *You must have to be quiet with someone else—and then it works.*

"Okay," I told Cary. "I'll have a quiet time with you."

"Great!" Cary replied. "Oh, and Larry is going to join us too."

Hmmm, I thought. *This will be interesting—three guys sitting quietly next to each other.* Because my friendship with Larry was marked by jokes and laughter, I imagined that it would be hard for us to sit quietly next to each other. *But,* I thought, *these guys seem legit, so I will definitely give it a shot.*

Cary added, "I'll come by your room at 6:30 tomorrow morning, and we can have our quiet time downstairs and then go to breakfast." I was shocked that I was going to be doing anything at 6:30 in the morning, but I told Cary, "Okay, I'll be ready."

The next morning—at 6:30—I answered the knock on my

door, and as I walked out, Cary said, "Where's your Bible?" A bit red-faced, I went back in and grabbed my big brown Bible. On the way downstairs, I scolded myself for not figuring out earlier that the Bible would obviously have something to do with a quiet time!

After we sat down in a corner of our cafeteria basement, Cary asked Larry to pray for our time. I remember being aware of God's presence with us as Larry prayed a short prayer with everyday words.

Next, Cary suggested that we read a short psalm out loud, so we each took turns reading a few verses. We talked for a few minutes about what we had just read, and then we each picked one verse as our favorite verse from the psalm.

Cary shared his verse, Larry shared his, and then it was my turn. I was so excited: I actually had a verse that stood out to me that morning! I was aware of not having to borrow something I had heard from someone else. I had personally read something directly from the Bible that stood out to my own mind and heart!

Cary went on and reminded us that the Bible says we should "be doers of the word, and not hearers only" (James 1:22, ESV). So we all agreed that we should pick one specific thing we would do that day because of what we had just read.

Again, Cary shared what he would do, Larry shared, and then I did too. I was cool on the outside but bursting on the inside, as I actually had a specific thing I could do that day because of what I had read in the Bible.

We went on and each prayed briefly, thanking God for

what He had talked to us about during our time together with Him. We also prayed for the day ahead. We spent no more than twenty-five minutes huddled together before we left those chairs and went back upstairs.

I was so excited that I practically floated to breakfast! I had just had a genuine, bona fide quiet time! I was conscious of having met with the living God. I was aware of not putting any energy into trying to be religious or spiritual or holy. I was just being me—and I, along with a couple other men, had actually just met with God!

That morning changed my life.

It's about a Relationship

Ever since that morning, I have cultivated the habit of having a daily quiet time. I did not start having a bunch of mystical experiences, and I did not merely add a spiritual discipline to my life. No! What was really life-changing was that I started pursuing my relationship with God.

In John 17:3, Jesus prayed, "This is eternal life, that they know you, the only true God, and Jesus Christ whom you have sent" (ESV). The word *know* in that verse comes from the Greek word *ginosko*, which implies personal experience and relationship. Jesus said that eternal life is not just something that happens when we die or when we "say a prayer" or when we are baptized. No, Jesus spoke of His followers having an actual relationship with the Father and with Him.

Essential Ingredients in Developing a Relationship

In your life, you have probably discovered that there are some essential ingredients that are required in developing your relationships with other people. Here are some of the ingredients I have found:

Time. Any relationship takes time in order for it to grow and deepen. It would be completely unreasonable to expect that someone you just met would immediately be your confidante and good friend in life. A relationship like that takes time to develop.

Effort. Without both parties putting effort into a relationship, it's not going anywhere! What if you repeatedly showed up for dinner with your friend, but that friend was always backing out because they had better things to do? After a while, you would realize that you were the only one putting effort into the relationship.

Communication. Similarly, a relationship can only go so far if you never talk with each other. In any growing relationship, there is a lot of mutual listening, talking, and understanding. You will also likely find some storytelling, some words of advice, and some encouragement.

Shared experiences. As a relationship grows with a friend, a spouse, or a sibling, you will, over time, share some memorable experiences. You know that a relationship is deepening when you can say to each other, "Remember when . . ." It is likely that those memories will bring back the original emotions of joy, sorrow, fear, or laughter. Hearts are often bonded together through shared experiences of life.

Essential Ingredients in Developing Your Relationship with God

Let me remind you that the God of the Bible is not a "force" or a "concept" or a "philosophy." As we saw in John 17:3, God is a person whose intention is to be known: He desires a relationship, and—think about this—He desires a deepening relationship with you!

Too many Christians think that an initial "introduction" to God is sufficient to have a relationship with Him. Now, meeting God for the first time is the most important thing someone could ever do! But imagine if all you ever did in life was shake people's hands and learn their names. You could hardly say that you really had relationships with all those people.

It is no different with God. He wants a relationship with you—and the ingredients in developing your relationship with Him are not that different from the ingredients in successful relationships with people.

If you want to have a deepening relationship with God, it will involve time, effort, communication, and shared experiences with Him.

And that is where quiet times fit in!

Having a quiet time with God is not an end in itself. Having a quiet time is really just a tool to help you develop and deepen your relationship with God.

What Is a Quiet Time?

Let's get a bit more concrete. A quiet time is time that you set aside to focus on God. Typically, a quiet time will involve talking with God (praying) and listening to God (reading the Bible). A basic outline for a daily quiet time involves:

Prayer. Talk with God about Him and about yourself.
Bible. Read and reflect on a passage in the Bible and
its implications for your life.
Prayer. Talk again with God about what you have read
and about the thoughts and intentions you have
formed based on what He has said in His Word.

Having a Spiritual Sandwich

One of my friends, Mike, calls this "having a spiritual sandwich." With the "bread" being prayer and the "meat" being God's Word, he got a number of us into the habit of asking each other, "Have you had your spiritual sandwich yet today?"

Here are some more specifics on how to use your time during your "spiritual sandwich":

Prayer

During your first round of prayer, use the ACTS guideline for prayer, but just focus on A and C at this point. (You'll focus on T and S during your second round of prayer.)

A—Adoration. Focus on praising God, adoring Him for who He is and what He is like. Almost every morning, I spend time quoting and praying over Lamentations 3:21-24 (NIV):

> Yet this I call to mind
>   and therefore I have hope:
>
> Because of the LORD's great love we are
>   not consumed,
>   for his compassions never fail.
> They are new every morning;
>   great is your faithfulness.
> I say to myself, "The LORD is my portion;
>   therefore I will wait for him."

The Holy Spirit uses this passage to whisper to me that God loves me and is faithful to His Word and to me. He gently points my mind and heart to the truth that every day He has new compassion for me. He reminds me that He is the portion I get in life, so I choose to trust in Him.

C—Confession. Confess any sins that you have not already confessed to Him. Now, don't waste time or energy "re-confessing" sins from last week or last year (or last decade!).

First John 1:9 declares, "If we confess our sins, he is faithful and just and will forgive us our sins and purify us from all unrighteousness" (NIV). What good news for us followers of Jesus! When we confess our sins to God, He completely forgives us and purifies us. We don't have to wait to "feel forgiven," nor do we need to "punish ourselves" for our sin. No—Jesus was punished for our sin instead! After we confess our sins to God, we can breathe a sigh of relief as we receive His forgiveness and then move on.

God's Word

During this time, do your "ABCs"! (Slightly juvenile, I know, but you'll remember it.)

A—Ask. Ask questions about what you are reading. Here are some of my favorite questions that I ask during my own quiet times:

> Who is saying this?
> To whom?
> Why?
> What was the writer's intent in saying this to his original audience?
> What were the original hearers likely thinking as they heard or read this?

> What is the main point in this passage?
> What can I apply to my life today from this passage?
> What does it seem that God is saying to me here?

B—Best Verse. As you read and ask questions, look for one verse in the passage on which you can "hang" the big lesson or truth you think God has been talking to you about. The "best verse" you choose might not be the verse that captures the theme of the passage you are reading; it is just the verse that sticks out most to you on that day. There are times when I have shared a quiet time with two or three other men, and we have all chosen a different "best verse."

As I go through my day, I will sometimes return to that "best verse," perhaps rereading it or just taking a few seconds to talk with God about it. Often, the Holy Spirit will bring it to mind in the middle of an unexpected situation. It's in that situation that I especially see the relevance of the verse to my life.

C—Commit. Choose one area of your life—or some part of your upcoming day—that you can commit to God. It might be a sales call or a presentation or a test or a meeting with a particular person. What is it about your "best verse" that resonates with your life? Commit that to God.

Sometimes what we commit to God is an attitude of the heart: "Today, Lord, I trust You with this." Sometimes it is a specific action we should take: "Yes, Lord, I will go to her and ask her forgiveness."

Prayer

Now, use the ACTS guideline to pray again, this time focusing on T and S.

T—Thanksgiving. Thank God for what He spoke to you. Thank Him for your "best verse" and for the truth or lesson that He talked to you about. This is also a good time to thank Him for other things, such as your job, your family, your coworkers, your home or apartment—even your struggles and hardships—and for how God wants to use those in your life.

S—Supplication. To "supplicate" is to ask, so this is time you can use to ask God for anything you need. You might ask Him for His help with your latest project or for patience with your coworker or for eyes to see your day the way He sees it. I will often ask God for wisdom in dealing with the situations and challenges I am facing, for help in resisting temptation, and for patience with others.

Planning Well for Your Daily Quiet Time

Over years of helping men and women establish the habit of developing their relationship with God, I have found that planning well for a quiet time helps almost everyone. Here are some things that can help you plan well:

Time

Find a good time of day to have your quiet time. Mark 1:35 says, "Very early in the morning, while it was still dark, Jesus got up, left the house and went off to a solitary place, where he prayed" (NIV). As a student, I began the habit of spending time with God every morning. For a while, I thought, *Surely the morning is the most "spiritual time" to have a quiet time.* Wrong! I think the principle is that Jesus, as busy as He was, did indeed carve out *some* time to be with His Father.

Beyond that, I think it wise to give some of your *best* time to meeting with God.

As a "morning person," my best time is in the morning. My son Tim is a "night person." When I am barely functioning at the end of the day, Tim is revving up. When he visits us these days, I will be crawling up the stairs to bed, only to see Tim sitting in his room, wide awake, having his "spiritual sandwich"! (It's pretty much a guarantee that if I tried to meet with God after 10:00 p.m., I would have a very quiet time—because I would quickly fall asleep!)

The best time of your day is likely the time in which you can be most present with Him—the time you can be focused, free of distractions, and totally attentive to Him.

Often, it is also helpful to choose a consistent time of day to meet with God. Whether it's morning, evening, right before lunch, or right after you get home from work, having a consistent daily time with God will help you make a daily quiet time a healthy habit.

Place

This might not be as important for everyone as it is for me, but it does help me to have a regular place for my quiet time. In the verse we just looked at, we read that Jesus went to "a solitary place" to talk with His Father.

In my home, I most often sit in the large overstuffed chair in our family room. I like that chair because it is right by our fireplace and a large picture window. Because I know I will sit there to meet with God in the morning, I will often place my Bible (which is on my iPhone), my journal, and a pen on the arm of the chair before I go to bed. (That prevents me from spending five minutes looking for those items in the morning.)

For you, it might be at your desk, on the train to work, in your car, or in a coffee shop. You might not be as obsessive as I am in all this, but I think it will help you to have it figured out beforehand so you can jump right in and not waste time deciding where to meet with God.

Plan

Early on, I discovered that if I did not know what I was going to read in God's Word for my quiet time, I could spend ten or more minutes trying to decide what to read. (Add that to five minutes of looking for my Bible and deciding where to sit and, well . . . you get the idea of how futile that scenario is!)

So now I usually decide in advance what in the Bible I am going to read. This month I am reading through 1 Peter in my quiet times. Today I read and reflected on the last few verses of chapter 2. Guess what I am reading tomorrow? That's right—the first few paragraphs of chapter 3. I don't have to debate it in my mind or hunt around for some other passage. It's already decided. So when I sit down, I just start where I left off yesterday.

It also helps me to decide if my time in God's Word will be for depth or breadth. If I am reading for depth, I will usually read just a few paragraphs a day. Sometimes I will even read the same few paragraphs several days in a row. I try not to move on to the next set of paragraphs until I sense that I have all that God wants to give me from that passage.

When I read for breadth, it is likely that I will read three or more chapters a day, usually as part of one of the many Bible reading plans that are now available online.

Where Should I Start?

If the idea of having a daily quiet time is new for you, here are a few suggestions:

> Spend your first quiet time reading Psalm 1.

> After that, pick one of the Gospels (Matthew, Mark, Luke, or John) for your daily quiet time. Decide to read a chapter a day—or a story a day. If you like action, start with the Gospel of Mark. If you like a lot of deep truths, start with John. If you like a lot of little details here and there, read Luke or Matthew.

> Next, read through Acts, which is the story of Christ's followers after He died, was resurrected, and ascended to heaven.

> At some point, especially if you have never done it, pick a Bible reading plan and read through the Bible. My friend Tom does this several times a year. When I graduated from college and started working as an office manager, I read through the Bible several times. I still like to read through the Bible every few years. It always helps me, mostly because seeing the big picture of the whole story gives me a context for the individual books, chapters, and paragraphs I read when I am going for depth.

What Is the Best Length of Time for a Quiet Time?

This is actually a trick question! There is no "correct" length of time for a quiet time. My initial quiet times, when I was a student, would last about fifteen minutes. Gradually they built up to about thirty minutes, which was broken down into an initial three or four minutes in prayer, about twenty minutes reading and reflecting, and then another five or six minutes praying again.

Then, when I worked in one of my management positions (sometimes for sixty hours a week) a few years after college, my quiet times shortened to about fifteen minutes again. When we had three young sons at home, my wife, Nancy, and I would take turns caring for our sons so that each of us could have a quiet time. If we each got thirty minutes in those days, it was a good day.

Some of my twentysomething friends today have long commutes, so their quiet times often involve a few minutes of prayer before they head out the door, and then they listen to an audio Bible as they drive or take the train into the city. Sometimes the first thing they do at work is write in their journal and pray through their day.

What If My Quiet Times Are Boring?

I have had several friends ask me about this. And I have had some boring quiet times myself! The reality is that most relationships, even if they start out full of excitement, newness, and maybe even passion, will settle down into a sort of "everydayness"—a relationship marked more by comfortable familiarity than by drama and thrill.

It is the same in our relationship with God. What started as a time of great excitement and lots of new lessons might now feel slightly more predictable. Not that God is ever "predictable" or "tame," but as we get to know Him, we can begin to anticipate what His Word says and teaches us. We grow more comfortable in knowing Him and in being known by Him.

In Psalm 16:11, the psalmist wrote, "In your presence there is fullness of joy" (ESV). Sometimes just being with someone is enough. Sometimes you don't need to say very much because there is joy in just being together. When I am feeling a little bored in my quiet time, I remind myself of this verse and of the truth that just being with God is wonderful, even if He has nothing brand-new to tell me.

If you have already established the habit of having a daily quiet time, you know that you can benefit from "mixing it up" a bit. Sometimes I just review verses I have memorized for my quiet time. Other times I simply listen to worship music. Sometimes I just walk and pray. No matter what I actually do on a given day, I want to fully enter into God's presence and experience His nearness. Remember: The main idea is to focus on your relationship with Him.

What If I Am Just Too Busy to Have a Daily Quiet Time?

Busyness happens! We all have busy days and busy seasons of life. All of us have had days that started off too late—or too early—when we were barely able to whisper a prayer to God, let alone have a quiet time with Him. And then there are those days when, for some reason, the opportunity just escapes us, and we find that we only have time for five minutes alone with God.

When this happens, don't beat yourself up over it. And don't decide that because you missed a day, you might as well never try again.

On most days, we typically find time for the things that are important to us. The chances are that, with a little bit of desire

and effort, you will usually be able to find time for your daily
quiet time.

Quiet Times in Transitions

As you know, I learned how to have a quiet time as a student.
It was an adjustment for me to continue that discipline once I
started working full-time. Since then, I have both experienced
and observed that major life transitions can interrupt even our
healthiest disciplines, including having daily quiet times.

I have talked with many recent college graduates who have
shared with me how challenging it has been to continue the
habit of meeting with God every day. I remember one newly
graduated friend who told me that he was really struggling
in this area. As we talked about it, we discovered that he had
grown used to having a sixty- to ninety-minute daily quiet
time as a "busy" college student. Drilling down a bit more, it
was clear that his idea of a daily time with God included getting a cup of coffee, relaxing a bit, answering some e-mails,
checking sports scores, and having a "spiritual sandwich" in
there somewhere.

His problem was that he was trying to mimic what he did
in college. As he focused on just being with God and not doing
all the "extras," he found that he could genuinely meet with
God for about twenty minutes every day. As he experimented
with different times of day and different quiet time methods,

he gradually eased into a new pattern of meeting with God that fit his new season of life.

Whether your transition involves being new to the workforce, being newly married, having a baby, or living in a new city, give yourself room to experiment with the best time, place, and manner for you to have your quiet time. Through it all, don't forget that your main goal is simply to be with God.

Just a Tool

Whether you call having a quiet time a "daily devotional," a "morning watch," or "time with God," this discipline is just a tool that helps you intentionally spend time with God so that you can deepen your relationship with Him.

It's the same with the other practical helps I have shared, such as praying through ACTS, having a "spiritual sandwich," and working through the "ABCs." All of them are just tools. They are not intended to be things you must do every day for legalistic reasons. They can be very useful in your walk with Christ, but if doing any of these becomes your focus instead of focusing on Christ—well, that misses the point of it all!

Thirty-Day Challenge

Whether you are a busy professional, a homemaker, a student, or a pastor, I have a challenge for you. Share this essay and the ideas in it with a few of your friends. Then determine to each have a quiet time every day for thirty days in a row. (That's plenty of time to establish a habit.) If one of you misses a day, agree that you will all start over until each of you—together—reaches thirty days in a row. Once you achieve this goal, pick a way to celebrate with one another—maybe a dinner out, a fun night, a hike, or a time when you can share with each other what you have been experiencing in your relationship with God.

Your Next Steps

Well, there you go, my friend. My purpose in this essay has been to give you both a biblical foundation for having a daily quiet time and some practical ideas and helps. Whether the idea of having a daily quiet time is brand-new for you or a spiritual discipline you dabble in or practice regularly, I pray that you have found some help in taking your next steps in developing your relationship with God—the most important relationship in your life!

6

THE ONE-DIRECTION LIFE

Jean Fleming

Jean Fleming is an author and international speaker. She and her husband, Roger, served as Navigator staff in California, Korea, Okinawa, Arizona, Washington, and Colorado. "The One-Direction Life" was her plenary address at The Navigators National Staff Conference in 2015, under the title "The Choices We Make."

WHEN I WAS EIGHTEEN, I made a choice that's giving me a one-direction life.

I was a senior in high school attending a Young Life weekend. It was April 1959 at the Flanders Hotel in Ocean City, New Jersey, where I believed in the Lord Jesus Christ. I remember climbing on the bus afterward for the trip back to Maryland and sliding over to a window seat. The bus was noisy—there were kids singing "A Hundred Bottles of Beer on the Wall"—but I was in a bubble. I was having my first date with Jesus. That was the start of a lifelong affair of the heart.

For the first time I was coming to the Bible with a spiritual connection. I didn't know the terms *devotions* or "quiet time." Reading the Bible and praying weren't spiritual disciplines; they were a spiritual aphrodisiac. Sometime in my first year of college that heavy sense of God's presence faded. But I chose to keep coming back morning after morning for my date with the Lord.

Fast-forward about twelve years: Roger and I were married and living in Asia. We'd had three kids in four years. I was feeding lots of servicemen—had baby spit-up on my shoulder, and a fatigued brain bordering on hamburger. My date with Jesus looked very different—sometimes it was just a verse card on the arm of the rocking chair as I nursed a baby. Some days I missed it altogether. But it was still an affair of the heart.

I believe our choices shape us. For me there are two choices: the choice to keep the date with the Lord every day, and the choice to keep it an affair of the heart. I need to make those choices over and over again.

It's in my date with Jesus that I see Him. He tells me I am His and He is mine. It's in my date with Jesus that He reminds me I'm forgiven and blessed; that He measures success differently; that there are invisible realms; that my life is hidden in Him; and that where I am weak He is strong. It's in my date with Jesus that transformation begins from the inside out. It's in my date with Jesus that He gives me something fresh to give to the generations behind me.

I believe the choice to keep a daily date with Jesus has kept me from frittering my life away. I mentored a young moms group for fourteen years. One mom with a smoky southern twang and a master's degree said, "I get up thirty minutes before my kids—to do Pinterest." A second mom said, "Oh, I don't let myself do Pinterest until I get certain things done on my to-do list." The first mom said, "If I waited until I got those things done, I would never get to Pinterest." She's right: You must build your life around what is important to you. I believe our choices shape us.

I believe also that our choices reveal us. If I ask that young mom to put down her five highest values, Pinterest wouldn't be on the list. But it's Pinterest that gets her up in the morning. I believe my choices keep me honest. They help me see if what I say I value, I actually value.

This year Roger and I celebrated our fiftieth wedding anniversary. We celebrated in Hawaii on our way to visit our son, who lives in Japan. Roger and I are early risers even on vacation, but even so there were surfer boys out there straddling their boards when we got up in the morning. This intrigued me, because some Colorado high schools have instituted a later start time based on teen sleep studies (you remember teens like to sleep late). So what's happening here? First light and they were out there one morning before 6:00 a.m. I counted about thirty surfers waiting for the next good wave.

Now I'm assuming that their mothers did not nag them to get them up to surf! So what gets them up? Desire! It's an affair of the heart. I suspect that surfer boys never ask themselves if getting up early to surf is legalistic. Surfers know that desire and discipline feed one another. Surfers know that desire plus discipline equals delight.

I cannot create desire for God. That's a gift at the new birth. I can't create desire for God, but I can feed it. I can also drain it of its holy energy by neglect. When my desire for God is at low tide, I keep my date with Jesus in the same spirit with which I keep my wedding vows.

Andrew Murray wrote that desire and choice prove what a man is already and decide what he is to become. At age seventy-four, my energy level is diminished. Like you, I must choose where my time and my energy will go. But as I approach the finish line, one thing is clear to me: I will end up with the life that I've chosen. I have kept my morning date with Jesus almost every day for fifty-seven years. I can't tell you how grateful I am to the Lord that at eighteen I made a choice that's given me a one-direction life. This is not an achievement. It's a grace.

MAKING CHRIST KNOWN

7

WORK: WHERE LIFE AND CALLING MEET

Jerry White

Jerry White is international president emeritus of The Navigators. An engineer, professor, and air force general, he serves on the board of directors for the Christian Leadership Alliance and is the author of a number of books. "Work: Where Life and Calling Meet" was originally published in 2013.

EVERYONE GOES TO WORK, but not everyone likes what they do. We wrestle with the difference between making a living and making a life. What many people say to themselves on many days sounds something like this: "Love my work? Forget it. The real work of God is my Bible study, my worship at church, and sharing my faith with more boldness. The only reason I work is to put bread on the table, to get ahead, and to make enough money to do some fun things—even give some of it to God."

What's wrong with this picture? Am I supposed to spend 40 percent of my waking life doing something God has no interest in? All for the sake of money and survival?

I think not. God is interested in your entire life. All of it— your dating, your marriage, your sexuality, your friendships, your Bible reading, your physical exercise, your meals, and yes, your work. He has gifted you with special skills and abilities that He expects you to employ well. He wants you to be as excited about constructing a building, teaching sixth graders, working in the home, or doing an elderly woman's hair in a beauty shop as you are about Bible study and walking with Him.

Reflecting on the purpose of his life, Olympic champion Eric Liddell, who was depicted in the movie *Chariots of Fire*, said, "I believe God made me for a purpose, but He also made me fast. And when I run, I feel His pleasure." He saw divine purpose in his missionary work in China *and* in his running. He lived out his spiritual conviction by rejoicing in his accomplishments on the track, by taking a moral stand when necessary, and by using his accomplishments as an avenue for sharing his faith in Jesus.

The idea that all of life is sacred, especially our work, is not heresy. It reflects the profound teaching of the Bible. In the rest of this booklet, we will explore these statements:

1. Work is divinely established by God.
2. Work is holy, not secular.
3. Work is your place of ministry and serving God.
4. Work is a calling, not a demand.
5. We are called to influence our work environment.
6. We are called to influence individuals.
7. Excellence, competence, and faithfulness are the keys to success.
8. Work is not simple or easy.

9. Work develops your character.
10. Money is good. Greed is not.

Work is divinely established by God.

The Garden of Eden was a farm, not Disneyland. In the beginning of time, God established two institutions: work and marriage. The Bible states, "For this reason a man shall leave his father and his mother, and be joined to his wife; and they shall become one flesh" (Genesis 2:24, NASB). God made marriage a divine, human institution, not a strictly Christian institution. It is for all humanity. It was made for procreation, pleasure, and companionship.

But earlier in that chapter, before the creation of woman, God made the Garden of Eden and assigned Adam to tend it: "The LORD God took the man and put him in the Garden of Eden to work it and take care of it" (Genesis 2:15, NIV).

Both institutions preceded the Fall and the entrance of sin into the world (Genesis 3:1-24). As a result of the Fall, marriage and childbirth became difficult, and work became hard; marriage and family, even with their blessings and pleasures, have become a source of pain and brokenness, and work in all fields has become more difficult. But both institutions are still part of His plan. Today, work can be unfulfilling and full of drudgery, but God did not intend for it to be like that. He meant for work to tap into our creative selves, to provide for the family, to care for the world, and to be a place of community.

In giving the Ten Commandments, God said, "Six days you shall labor and do all your work, but the seventh day is a sabbath [rest]" (Exodus 20:9-10, NASB). Notice that it says, "Six days you shall labor." This was a command to work, not just a command to rest.

God ordained work and wants us to love it.

Work is holy, not secular.

There is a myth that there are two kinds of work: sacred and secular. In the sacred camp, we put priests, pastors, youth workers, missionaries, people who are reaching the downtrodden, and others whose jobs seem to be religious in nature. Then we lump all other workers into the secular camp: carpenters, nurses, engineers, factory workers, sales people, military personnel, lawyers, homemakers, and so on. In the Old Testament, there was a division of duties between priests and others. In the New Testament, this was erased. Colossians 3:23 states, "Whatever you do, work at it with all your heart, as working for the Lord, not for men" (NIV).

Following this myth leads to the notion that there is a "higher calling"; that is, that you are serving God more as a pastor or missionary than you are as a truck driver or an accountant. From that concept comes the strange idea that God blesses one more than the other.

Mark Greene of the U.K. wrote this about the "Sacred/Secular Divide":

> [It] leads us to believe that really holy people become missionaries, moderately holy people become pastors and people who aren't much use to God get a job. Bah, Humbug. . . . The reality is that the majority of Christians do have a sense that they are second-class citizens of the kingdom of heaven and that the 110 waking hours they spend in non-church activities each week are not of any substantial interest to the one who created the world He calls us to steward. . . . [The sacred/secular divide] tells us that all Christians may be born equal, but full-time Christian workers are more equal than others. It's a lie. Did Jesus call any of us to be a part-time Christian worker?[1]

God is present in every part of our lives—equally. Every part of a believer's life is sacred. We might work with people who have a secular mind-set, but it is not a secular job for us. For us, all of life is "holy ground."

Work is your place of ministry and serving God.
Ministry is a very misunderstood word. So many associate it with a religious profession rather than its root meaning of "service." Others associate the word with certain spiritual activities such

as Bible study, helping the poor, or teaching a class at church. Consider how Paul addressed the issue of work:

> Make it your ambition to lead a quiet life, to mind
> your own business and to work with your hands,
> just as we told you, so that your daily life may win
> the respect of outsiders and so that you will not be
> dependent on anybody.
>
> I THESSALONIANS 4:11-12, NIV

In this Scripture, we see that we are to earn our own way, have a good reputation with the people around us, and provide for the needs of our family.

The context is work. God put us in this context for more than one purpose. Our "ministry" has two equally valid parts: We are there to "do good" *and* to demonstrate the presence of Christ to the people around us. We are not just looking for ways to "serve God" in the evenings and on weekends. We are serving God now in our workplace as well as in all the other parts of our lives.

In my lifetime, I have had the privilege of serving as the international president of The Navigators. My wife, Mary, and I, by God's grace, have been personally involved with many individuals as they have come to know and walk with Christ. But I am *equally* proud of my thirty-seven years of service to our country with the U.S. Air Force. I view all of it as ministry and service to God.

Work is a calling, not a demand.

Studs Terkel, famous author of the common man, once quoted Nora Watson, a writer of health-care literature, saying, "I think most of us are looking for a calling, not a job."[2]

People ask me about my calling, expecting me to respond that I am called to The Navigators. But I believe that God equally called me to the U.S. Air Force. In that context I worked as an engineer, professor, and general. At the time, I did not fully comprehend it as a calling. But in retrospect, it is clear that God called Mary and me to live the life of Christ in the air force. One retired four-star general, who was my commander, recently put his arm around me at a social gathering and said, "Jerry was my reserve assistant. But really he is my spiritual mentor." As I taught at the Air Force Academy, several fellow faculty members came to faith even though I had thought I was there to teach and reach students (which also happened).

The other part of my calling is the work itself. During my time in the air force, I served as a mission controller at Cape Canaveral, taught astronautics at the Air Force Academy, coauthored a textbook, and served as the mobilization assistant to the commander of Air Force Materiel Command before retiring at the rank of major general. These tasks were also part of my calling. Through them, I also served God.

As Paul interacted with believers in Corinth, he said, "Friends, stay where you were called to be. God is there. Hold the high ground with him at your side" (1 Corinthians 7:24, MSG). He considered their current situation God's calling. We are not to look for "greener grass" somewhere else. That doesn't mean God will not direct us to another job or calling at some point. It simply means that God has called us to where we are now. God calls us to the type of work we do and to the place of our work. With each move or change of job, Mary and I had to seek direction from God. Early in my career, I encountered a number of changes and opportunities. But in each change, it was clear that this was where God had called me and where He wanted me to be.

We are called to influence our work environment.

Imagine a "church" where you arrive at 7:30 in the morning. You stay all day talking with people, working on projects, and giving reports on your assignments. You encounter people who make you mad, who lie to you and even debate whether your project is going in the right direction. No one prays—it is not allowed in this place. There is no preaching or music (except for a few who bob their heads up and down to the music on their headphones). You cannot leave until at least 5:00 or 5:30 p.m., depending on how your project is going. And this "church" is five days a week. Sometimes more.

You come in one day and find that one of your friends has been "excommunicated," forbidden to return. You are upset and concerned, so you call her. But the experience is too hurtful, and she doesn't want to talk—at least not at the moment. But finally she agrees to meet after "church"—at a nearby pub. You and a couple of friends sit there, talk with her, and commiserate about what to do now that she can't come to your particular "church." You brainstorm on another that might fit her needs. Then you talk about a few others who will be asked to leave because there is a shrinking demand for the product they were working on.

Is this a strange church? You bet. However, I am describing our workplace and your work. In one sense, it is your church and congregation. Even though God might not be mentioned at work, the Bible teaches that He is everywhere in it—He is omnipresent. Because we are called to be His priests (1 Peter 2:9) and because our work is a form of worship, valuable to God and part of His grand plan for men and women in fulfilling His purposes, it is our responsibility to work for the transformation of our workplaces. Just as we would not tolerate the above behavior in our local congregation of believers, so, as God's "salt and light," we must do what we can to see our workplaces changed.

Salt gives flavor and savor to the food. In larger quantities, it also preserves. And it makes a person thirsty. We need to add flavor to our workplaces and society, to preserve them by our integrity and to cause people to thirst for the life that we have in Christ. Jesus describes us as light. We don't cover up our faith. Rather, we let it show in appropriate ways: by our work, our character, and our words. In these ways, no matter if we are in authority or occupy the lowest part in the hierarchy, we can influence our work environments.

We are called to influence individuals.

I am often asked how to be a witness for Christ in the workplace. It is not simple. The extremes range from being overly aggressive and even offensive to being so silent that no one even knows you are a follower of Christ. Neither extreme is good. Here are some lessons I have learned and practiced in my life:[3]

> Be part of the social environment. Go to parties. Be on work-sponsored athletic teams. Accept invitations to birthdays and family events or for meals in homes.
> Know your coworkers. Learn their interests, birthdays, anniversaries, background, and children's names.
> Listen. Take your coworkers seriously.
> Meet needs. Be alert to illnesses, death of a parent, or difficult issues with children or family.
> Pray regularly for coworkers by name.
> Introduce them to the Bible at the appropriate time.
> Know how to share your personal testimony and the gospel.
> Be competent in your work.
> Don't take work time to witness to people.
> Keep in touch even when you leave a job.
> Don't argue. Simply help people discover answers to their questions.

**Excellence, competence, and faithfulness
are the keys to success.**

Everyone wants to succeed. We certainly don't want to fail. Yet
not everyone ends up being the CEO, the owner, or the boss.
Not everyone gets promoted and rewarded, but everyone can be
respected in their work. In my work experience, I have found
certain keys to doing well—not a guarantee or a magic potion
but elements that will gain respect.

Excellence

Jesus worked as a carpenter. Paul worked as a tentmaker. Peter
worked as a fisherman. Lydia worked as a cloth-dyer. Each did
their work with excellence. They did their work "heartily, as for
the Lord and not for people" (Colossians 3:23, NASB). Their work
reflected who they were. The book of Proverbs explains it like this:

> I went past the field of the sluggard,
> > past the vineyard of the man who lacks judgment;
> thorns had come up everywhere,
> > the ground was covered with weeds,
> > and the stone wall was in ruins.
> I applied my heart to what I observed
> > and learned a lesson from what I saw:
> A little sleep, a little slumber,
> > a little folding of the hands to rest—
> and poverty will come on you like a bandit
> > and scarcity like an armed man.

PROVERBS 24:30-34, NIV

Working with excellence draws attention for good. Laziness or sloppiness builds a reputation of one who is a poor worker. Have you ever heard comments like these?

> "I'd rather deal with the non-Christians in business. Too many Christians have really disappointed me in their dealings."
> "He might be a Christian, but he really doesn't do good work."
> "She claims to be a Christian, but I know atheists who work harder and do better work than she does."

We don't want to be like that. Yes, many non-believers also do poor work. But we are upholding the reputation of Christ.

Excellence is not perfection. If it were, I would be in deep trouble. It does mean doing your work to the best of your ability and working hard at it. One of my first jobs as a teen was working in a seed store. I was to bag grass seed in five-pound bags. I labored to make it five pounds on an old weight arm scale, putting in seed and taking it out until it was "perfect." My boss weighed the bags and found that all were slightly less than five pounds. He almost fired me. Instead, he showed me how to do it—how to fill the bag till the scale tipped at five pounds and then add a little more to be sure it favored the customer. My "perfection" was not appreciated. Excellence required that I give a little more.

Competence

Competence is different than excellence. Competence means having suitable or sufficient skill, knowledge, and experience for some purpose. It means being properly qualified and speaks of our level of skill and ability to perform. Again, Proverbs describes it well: "Do you see a man skilled in his work? He will serve before kings; he will not serve before obscure men" (Proverbs 22:29, NIV).

Moses did not hire the cheapest workers when he built the tabernacle in the Old Testament. He hired the best. Speaking of a man named Bezalel, Moses described him as someone "with the Spirit of God, with skill, ability and knowledge in all kinds of crafts—to make artistic designs for work in gold, silver and bronze, to cut and set stones, to work in wood and to engage in all kinds of artistic craftsmanship" (Exodus 35:31-33, NIV). To work with Bezalel, "Moses summoned . . . every skilled person to whom the LORD had given ability and who was willing to come and do the work" (Exodus 36:2, NIV).

God gave people skill and ability. Yet they had to be willing to come and work. It is the same with each of us. We are given talent, but we must develop it and be willing to use it. The people who built the tabernacle had to work hard to become skillful and competent.

My advice is to get training and education and obtain knowledge to become competent. But remember that you cannot be competent at everything. We each have specific skills and limitations. We should not be embarrassed or discouraged that we do not possess certain skills. Early in my career, I discerned that I was not a natural researcher in my field. I was a doer. I worked best at leading. With great effort, I was able to do research, but it was not natural for me. We need to do good self-assessment and develop skills in the areas where God has given us talent. When we are younger, a major task is to understand our skills and limitations. Try many things. But strive for competence in what you do.

Faithfulness

Can people depend on you? Do you do what you say you will do? Can you meet deadlines? Proverbs describes this graphically: "Like a bad tooth or a lame foot is reliance on the unfaithful in times of trouble" (Proverbs 25:19, NIV).

As people worked for me, I would share with them that one of my highest values was that they did what they said they would do. If they could not, they should let me know or ask for help. I communicated that the only real failure was to say they would do something and then not do it. Employers and supervisors need to know that they can count on you. In many ways, faithfulness trumps competence.

The combination of excellence, competence, and faithfulness will pave the way for advancement and promotion, for better service to others, for reputation, and for your witness for Christ. Beyond this, you will develop self-assurance and confidence. Jesus compared a faithful and an unfaithful worker in this way:

The one who is faithful in a very little thing is also faithful in much; and the one who is unrighteous in a very little thing is also unrighteous in much. Therefore if you have not been faithful in the use of unrighteous wealth, who will entrust the true wealth to you? And if you have not been faithful in the use of that which is another's, who will give you that which is your own?

LUKE 16:10-12, NASB

In the following parable Jesus explained to His disciples how faithfulness serves God and others:

And the Lord replied, "I'm talking to any faithful, sensible man whose master gives him the responsibility of feeding the other servants. If his master returns and finds that he has done a good job, there will be a reward—his master will put him in charge of all he owns.

"But if the man begins to think, 'My Lord won't be back for a long time,' and begins to whip the men and women he is supposed to protect, and to spend his time at drinking parties and in drunkenness—well, his master will return without notice and remove him from his position of trust and assign him to the place of the unfaithful."

LUKE 12:42-46, TLB

Jesus taught faithfulness and dependability. He meant this both in terms of our faithfulness to Him and our reputation as a worker.

Work is not simple or easy.

This leads us to the fact that God has not promised ease in our work. When I first became a mission controller at Cape Canaveral in the space program, I was intimidated. I felt inadequate. I had a degree in electrical engineering, and yet I did not understand much of what was going on. I hung on by my fingernails. My fellow controllers were older, had master's degrees, and just seemed smarter. But I learned, went to seminars, worked hard, and asked lots of questions. Each week we would brief the launch schedule to about fifty project managers who were vying for the best schedule for their programs. When we didn't give them what they had asked for, debate and questions flew around the room. The first time I led this meeting as a twenty-three-year-old lieutenant, I had worked like crazy to be prepared, comforted by the knowledge that my boss would be there to rescue me when I got in trouble. I began the briefing, and to my consternation my boss got up and left the room—and fed me to the wolves! I had to learn quickly.

You might be in over your head. You might be embarrassed. You might fail, as I did in my early career, when I was planning to be a pilot. You might lose sleep as you struggle to learn skills to survive. But being challenged is no reason to stop trying. As

WORK: WHERE LIFE AND CALLING MEET

one proverb says, "One who is slack in his work is brother to one who destroys" (Proverbs 18:9, NIV).

Being a good worker, especially when it is not easy, gives personal satisfaction and establishes a good reputation as a follower of Christ. I have always been challenged by Proverbs 6:9-11 (MSG):

> So how long are you going to laze around doing nothing?
>> How long before you get out of bed?
> A nap here, a nap there, a day off here, a day off there,
>> sit back, take it easy—do you know what comes next?
> Just this: You can look forward to a dirt-poor life,
>> poverty your permanent houseguest!

I knew I didn't want to be like that.

Another factor that makes work difficult is the pressure just to survive; it takes hard work to provide for yourself and harder work to provide for a family. Proverbs acknowledges this struggle: "The laborer's appetite works for him; his hunger drives him on" (Proverbs 16:26, NIV).

Despite the pressure, this passage teaches that it is good to be motivated by "having to put bread on the table" and supporting one's family. My stepfather was a truck driver. He never complained when he had to work the docks "throwing freight" into the trucks. Even at age sixty-two, he had to produce like the twenty-three-year-olds in similar jobs. He was glad to have a job. What was going on in his mind, I do not know. I just know that he did not complain in my hearing. It was not easy.

If we are looking for ease, we won't find much encouragement from God.

Work develops your character.

God uses work to cause us to depend on Him and to develop areas of character—like patience, faithfulness, love, honor, purity, and integrity. In work, we find challenges to all of these essential characteristics of a godly person. How we work says much about who we are. It is part of God's refining process in our lives. In work, we suffer, are treated unfairly, are tempted to cut corners and disparage our competitors. How we handle those urges and temptations builds our inner self. When we are honest and do not get the sale, we pay a price. When we admit we made a mistake and get a bad review, we learn the peace of living with a clear conscience. When we are maligned by a coworker and do not respond in kind, we might suffer in the short term, but we will grow and earn respect in the end.

In the air force, I heard there was a person being considered for a key senior position that I was to be offered. Though there were opportunities to "campaign" against this person, I said nothing and was given the position. Later I met this person, and today he is a very good friend of mine in my air-force community. In another instance, I had quietly criticized a senior leader—I did not like him at all. Then, at a social event (where

I usually avoided him), he told me that he had received Christ as a youth and reads his Bible daily. I was embarrassed by my thoughts and feelings. Both experiences provided opportunities to grow in character.

Sometimes the challenges to our character come not from our own mistakes but from somebody else's. One friend was passed over for promotion to a senior rank, largely because of being a follower of Christ. The person who had written his negative evaluation later recognized how unfair he had been. A year later, he backed my friend fully in a new round of promotions—and he was promoted. But the intervening year was humbling and miserable. He grew immensely in his character.

Character development generally is not enjoyable. Yet we emerge a better, more complete person: "For you, O God, tested us; you refined us like silver" (Psalm 66:10, NIV).

Money is good. Greed is not.

Work brings us money. Some jobs bring little, while others bring much. Taking a position because it pays well is not evil, but it should also not be the major reason we accept a position. When we have much, we can be more generous. Wealth can purify us, if we choose to use it well, or corrupt us. We choose which. Work provides us with opportunities to make wealth, buy a nice car, and move into a bigger home. But especially it allows us the choice of being generous and giving to worthy causes for the sake of God's kingdom. The wise man Agur said to God, "Give me neither poverty nor riches, but give me only my daily bread. Otherwise, I may have too much and disown you and say, 'Who is the LORD?' Or I may become poor and steal, and so dishonor the name of my God" (Proverbs 30:8-9, NIV).

Likewise, Paul instructed his friend and disciple Timothy about money:

> But godliness with contentment is great gain. For we brought nothing into the world, and we can take nothing out of it. But if we have food and clothing, we will be content with that. People who want to get rich fall into temptation and a trap and into many foolish and harmful desires that plunge men into ruin and destruction. For the love of money is a root of all kinds of evil. Some people, eager for money, have wandered from the faith and pierced themselves with many griefs.
>
> But you, man of God, flee from all this, and pursue righteousness, godliness, faith, love, endurance and gentleness. . . .
>
> Command those who are rich in this present world not to be arrogant nor to put their hope in wealth, which is so uncertain, but to put their hope in God, who richly provides us with everything for our enjoyment. Command them to do good, to be rich in good deeds, and to be generous and willing to share.
>
> 1 TIMOTHY 6:6-11, 17-18, NIV

In the Old Testament, Moses delivered this word to the people about how to view prosperity:

> You may say to yourself, "My power and the strength of my hands have produced this wealth for me." But remember the LORD your God, for it is he who gives you the ability to produce wealth, and so confirms his covenant, which he swore to your forefathers, as it is today.
>
> DEUTERONOMY 8:17-18, NIV

Money is good, the result of our labor. It is meant to be used for God and for good.

Conclusion: Work is a privilege.

Work is an integral part of our lives. It is part of God's design for us and His purposes in the world. It is the source of great joy and fulfillment when it is fully committed to God. Yet it is important to note that most of the people in the world are happy just to have a job at all. It is a privilege. Beyond that simple fact, there is pleasure in working. Loving what you do gives great satisfaction. There is legitimate fulfillment in it. "The sleep of a laborer is sweet, whether he eats little or much" (Ecclesiastes 5:12, NIV). It is fulfilling to know that you have worked hard, done your job well, and been deserving of your wages.

Your job might not be all that you want at this point in your life. Through the years, I have had boring jobs. I have had jobs I did not particularly enjoy. In fact, I consider it a plus if even 50 percent of the work I do in my job is exciting and fits my gifts. Some tasks just have to be done if you are part of a team and part of your company's production. Yet for all the reasons we have discussed, work is still a high calling.

This essay has mostly been about changing how you think about work. Here are three practical suggestions for putting this new thinking into practice:

1. *Study*. Find some materials, find a friend, and study the topic of work.[4] For a quick start, look at Genesis 1:28. What do these commands, added all up, say about work?

2. *Pray*. Pick a time and a place, and pray every day for a week about your work day. Pray for excellence, competence, and faithfulness.

3. *Do*. Pick a handful of the activities under "We are called to influence individuals" and do them.

Let us be people who live out our faith in the workplace.

8

TELLING HIS STORY BY TELLING YOURS

Joe Maschhoff

Joe Maschhoff leads the work of The Navigators in the Caribbean. Previously he served as the director of The Navigators' ministry to twenty-somethings and as a minister to college students in Southern California. "Telling His Story by Telling Yours" was first published in 2013.

I REGULARLY MEET PEOPLE who want to make a difference for Christ. They want to affect the world around them. They know that it somehow involves them verbalizing the gospel, and they suspect that they have opportunities to do so. They long to make a difference in the lives of the people they know, but they are unsure of what to do next or what it should look like.

One of the things we clearly need is the ability to articulate the gospel, specifically the facts and objective reality of the gospel. For a true conversion to take place, we know that at some point people's minds must be swayed toward the logic, facts, and truth of the gospel.

However, I have also found that often the path to true conversion must go through the wild and beautiful fields of the heart. For some, the facts of the gospel will have a strong influence on their heart. But for many others, the facts are only part of the equation.

Therefore, besides some skill in articulating the basic facts of the gospel, we also need some skill in sharing our own story, a story that will access people's hearts. I have found that the ability to tell our story is not often discussed. It doesn't seem to get as much press. But I have also found that it is critical. If we share the gospel without conversation or without relating it to real life, many of our friends often only hear religious information. This is particularly true with people we see often, such as in a work environment, a living situation, or with extended family.

This principle is true in many parts of life. Good marketing, for example, tells the potential customer about the product but also tells the customer about someone's experience with the product. Potential customers want to know if it works! "You bought the vacuum . . . so did it do the job? Was it all you hoped it would be?"

Likewise, in a courtroom a lawyer can tell the jury about the facts of a case, but it is often the testimony of witnesses that galvanizes a jury's verdict. Testimony gives color and life to the facts of a case. It brings it home.

So it is as we live among our coworkers, neighbors, fellow students, family, and friends and engage them about our faith.

They need to hear the facts of the gospel, but there is a natural urge inside of them to know: "Does it work? Are you really different because of it? How? Tell me about it." Hopefully, they already have some inkling from watching your life. But it is presumptuous to make that assumption. People will often need to be told. Additionally, we will have opportunities with people who do not know us as well (for example, someone we met on a plane, a new neighbor, or a friend from class).

If you have never tried it before, you might be surprised to find that many people, especially friends, are interested in hearing your story. There are probably more than you know who, if the circumstances were right, would be open to hearing your story about Jesus' redemptive work in your life.

I think that if I had never identified myself with Jesus in the office where I worked, most of my co-workers would have thought I was just a nice person. The same was true on my dorm floor in college. In both situations, it was important for me early on to reference the fact that I follow Jesus. My friends in college and those later in the workplace never forgot that point of identification. It marked me. As a child of God and as His ambassador, that is exactly what I wanted.

What did Jesus do?

Jesus could have exclusively told people facts and truth. He could have only passed on information. Instead, He chose to offer stories that would bring color to the information people needed so desperately. He chose to elaborate on the gospel by offering examples of what He was talking about.

In fact, He often started with a story. It was not unusual for Him to illustrate a point and then explain it later (sometimes much later!) with direct teaching.

When asked by some powerful religious people, "Who is my neighbor?" Jesus answered their question by telling the story of the Good Samaritan (Luke 10:29-36, NIV).

Matthew reported that Jesus "told them many things in parables" (Matthew 13:3, NIV). In that same passage, He made many of His points by starting with a story. He was ultimately after people's hearts, not just their minds, and the heart is often awakened by story.

Ultimately, people will need the facts of the gospel. When we stand before the King of kings, the facts are what will matter, yet story is often the highway we travel to discover and embrace facts.

Revelation 12 is a fascinating chapter in the Bible, with vivid imagery about the celestial battle that takes place between good and evil, between the Lamb of God and Satan. In verse 11, we read that Satan was overcome by two things: "They overcame him by the blood of the Lamb and by the word of their testimony" (NIV).

This passage teaches that we are the ones who will someday overcome the Evil One and that we are armed with two very powerful weapons. These are weapons that cannot be stopped: "the blood of the Lamb" and "the word of their testimony."

The facts of the gospel (such as the shed blood of the Lamb and the resurrected Christ) are certainly powerful enough for us. However, isn't it interesting that God mentions two powerful weapons here? It is not only the *facts* of the gospel but also "their testimony"—their *experience* of the gospel—that wins the day.

The story of our experience testifies to the power of the blood of the Lamb! Our testimony acts as a validation of the power of the gospel. People can reject the facts of the gospel and even its logic, but it is very hard to argue with someone about their *experience* of the gospel.

And this powerful tool is available to us all!

Jesus did not come to pass on a set of ideas. He came to deliver a reality-changing message. He came not just to relay information but to complete His great story, to sweep us up into His movement through history. Our stories are part of His.

Jesus came to bring validation and completeness to creation. He came to be a living testimony to the person of God—that He is real and that this life really does have purpose. Your story evidences these truths.

Jesus could have dropped a manual of rules and systems on us. Instead, He came and lived out an example. He put "flesh" on truth so that it could become understandable and digestible. He asked questions. He listened. He testified. He told stories. He listened more. He elaborated. He clarified. He spoke in examples, parables, and allegories. His goal, like the goal of all good communication, was not to deliver a message but to have His message understood.

Your story is like a precious diamond. It is radiant, it is undeniably beautiful, and it is priceless. Why is it so precious? It is because your story is really His story. He is eternally beautiful, and your story tells of how His beauty shows up in your life.

No evil can stand against your story.

Having embraced the reality of the gospel, you are covered by the blood of the Lamb. When that is combined *with your story*, you are unstoppable!

Not for me?

You might be thinking that this isn't for you. I understand and have been there.

I find that for those who do not engage others with their story, it seems there are three main reasons:

1. They are unconvinced that their story matters.
2. They think their story is boring.
3. They don't know how to engage others with it.

Let me take a shot at addressing these three objections, giving particular attention to the third.

Are you unconvinced that your story matters?

No one lives where you do, has the friends you do, goes to school where you do, works where you do—no one is you but you! You can trust that God has placed you in all these circumstances with great care and attention to detail, and He has done so in love.

God has sovereignly placed you right where you are. He wants you to be all that He intended. He wants you to thrive. He wants you to flourish. He wants to call greatness out of you.

A big part of that greatness is your being a life-giver to those you encounter. We give life to people in many ways—through acts of kindness, through our work, through encouragement, and also by identifying with and introducing others to the Source of all life.

It is very likely that no one can get through to your friends, neighbors, and coworkers like you can. Many do not want to come to a Christian meeting or a church service (not yet, anyway). You are the one planted among them. Having a direct influence on the eternal destiny of those you love is one of the greatest thrills of life!

It is a precious gift that God has given us to partner with Him in this endeavor of pointing others to Christ.

This great work among those who do not yet know Christ is not strictly for "them." It is not just for those religious all-stars "over there" in the mission field. It is for you, right where you are.

Do you think your story is boring?

In Isaiah 60:22, we see the value that God puts on those of us who think we are unimportant, small, or that our story is not very interesting: "The least of you will become a thousand, the smallest a mighty nation. I am the LORD" (NIV).

This verse, in modern language, could easily have been written as follows: "The most unexciting person with the most colorless story—he is the one I'll use because I am ME."

God values the seemingly small and unimportant—this

means that if you think you are either of those, you are actually in a good place. He does not see us as unimportant or small. He does not see our stories as pedestrian or boring, and neither should we. He happens to love the underdog, and He seems to love using small efforts to achieve great results.

Because He is the Lord and all-important, we don't have to be important. He is! That is His job. As children of the King, our importance is wrapped up in His. And remember, our story is really just part of His.

You have a story, and because of that, you are relevant, beloved, and useful.

You don't know how to engage others with it?

Wondering how to tell your story is a fair question and represents a significant reason for writing this essay. We often just need a little help. The next section will go into more detail, but let me say two things about learning the "how" before we get there.

One of the first things we need to learn is how to see the opportunities that are all around us for sharing our story. These opportunities might be with our neighbors, fellow students, coworkers, friends at the gym, old friends, immediate family, extended family, and the barista you have slowly gotten to know over the last several months.

We are constantly interacting with others. It is a great gift that God has given us because people are beautiful, and all of them—no matter how far they are from Christ—carry the image of God. Interacting with people is an incredibly God-like activity.

There will be moments with people that are opportunities. We only need to see them as such.

The second point is for those who have already learned things that work on campus. I began to learn how to share my story while in college, on my dorm floor. I was shocked to find out that when approached the right way, people wanted to hear my story (usually not in one sitting, though).

When I got a job in an office after college, I was very curious to find out if some of the same things I had learned in college carried over to the workplace. I found that they usually did, but there were some adjustments I had to make. My friends and coworkers were just as open to talking as my friends in college. So while you might need to make some adjustments, many of the things you have already learned on campus will also work off campus.

Whether on campus or in the workplace, I have found it rare that I have an opportunity to just "tell" my story in a monologue-type way. I have found it much more common that I have an opportunity to "converse" my story, specifically certain parts of it, with my friends. Here is another way to say it: There are times when I get to tell my whole story *to* people. It is far more common, though, that I get to communicate my story *with* people, a little bit at a time.

So how do I share it?

Remember, your story is like a precious diamond. There are many facets to it. It looks different depending on what "angle" you look at it from—you will share different things depending on your friend's perspective. It is also experienced differently depending on "lighting." (For example, sitting in a hospital waiting room is different from sitting in a coffee shop.) It also looks different depending on the viewer's attention to detail (because your friend is on his or her own spiritual journey).

We will often have chances to ask a question or two, listen, share a little, ask some more questions, listen more, then share more, and so on. All this can happen while in front of a football game, over coffee, or at lunch. We are communicating our story with a friend.

Sometimes we might have a few minutes at a bus stop with a stranger. Or we might have ten or so minutes in a conversation with a friend on the way to class or on a break at work. Other times we might have a few hours in a car with someone.

Though these situations might all be a little different, having some heart and just a little skill in being able to converse will help you tremendously. It is far more of an art than a science, and it will feel more comfortable the more you do it.

In John 4:4-18, 25-26 (NIV), Jesus models some important principles about telling our story. (In the following excerpt, I have used brackets to note a few principles that I want to make a few comments on later.)

Now he had to go through Samaria. So he came to a town in Samaria called Sychar, near the plot of ground Jacob had given to his son Joseph. Jacob's well was there, and Jesus, tired as he was from the journey, sat down by the well. It was about the sixth hour. *[1. Live your life.]*

When a Samaritan woman came to draw water, Jesus said to her, "Will you give me a drink?" (His disciples had gone into the town to buy food.) *[2. Go out of your way to treat others with dignity.]*

The Samaritan woman said to him, "You are a Jew and I am a Samaritan woman. How can you ask me for a drink?" (For Jews do not associate with Samaritans.)

Jesus answered her, "If you knew the gift of God and who it is that asks you for a drink, you would have asked him and he would have given you living water." *[3. Be alert for opportunities to go deeper with them.]*

"Sir," the woman said, "you have nothing to draw with and the well is deep. Where can you get this living water? Are you greater than our father Jacob, who gave us the well and drank from it himself, as did also his sons and his flocks and herds?" *[4. Listen well.]*

Jesus answered, "Everyone who drinks this water will be thirsty again, but whoever drinks the water I give him will never thirst. Indeed, the water I give him will become in him a spring of water welling up to eternal life." *[5. Share your story, but leave room for conversation.]*

The woman said to him, "Sir, give me this water so that I won't get thirsty and have to keep coming here to draw water."

He told her, "Go, call your husband and come back."

"I have no husband," she replied. *[6. Stop telling your story when it leads into other people telling theirs.]*

Jesus said to her, "You are right when you say you have no husband. The fact is, you have had five husbands, and the man you now have is not your husband. What you have just said is quite true." . . . *[7. Enter into their story.]*

The woman said, "I know that Messiah" (called Christ) "is coming. When he comes, he will explain everything to us."

Then Jesus declared, "I who speak to you am he." *[8. Share truth, but don't be concerned if you can't get into the whole thing yet.]*

1. Live your life. Jesus was tired and thirsty. He was living real life, had a real need, and was on a real journey. He asked a Samaritan woman for help with His need. He came across this woman on a natural pathway of life. Yet it is clear from the story that He was ready to engage and was paying attention to opportunities that would show up.

2. Go out of your way to treat others with dignity. Almost immediately, Jesus distinguished Himself from other weary Jewish travelers just by engaging with this Samaritan woman. By talking with her, Jesus was showing her respect; this was a time when, because of a deeply ingrained superiority complex,

Jews did not relate to Samaritans. Jesus showed respect just by talking with this woman. It was a way that was unique without being pushy. She knew that He was different because people just didn't show that much respect. But He did!

3. Be alert for opportunities to go deeper with them. Jesus and the Samaritan woman shared a few comments about water because fetching water is what they were doing; that is why they both found themselves in that location at the same time. There was a real opportunity there. Water was a natural thing to discuss. Jesus was not lost in some religious fantasy world with her. He was really there by that well in real life and was really tired and really thirsty. By now, she knew that He was a different kind of person, one who actually showed some interest in her well-being, so it was not hard for her to enter into dialogue that was a little deeper. An opportunity was there.

4. Listen well. There is a time for direct spiritual conversation about the core facts of the gospel and a time for us to share our story. In this story, that is not what happened. Jesus' whole posture was one of listening, asking good questions, and then commenting in a relevant way. He didn't "dump-truck" her with information.

5. Share your story, but leave room for conversation. Notice that even in this short conversation, He was not preaching at her. He told God's story to her by telling her a little bit about Himself. He actually didn't even tell her very much, but just enough. There was room for them to talk about it. They were relating. As we all know, there are many interesting things about

Jesus. But He didn't cover all of them. He only testified to what was relevant and helpful to her. He showed her a facet of His life that would matter to her. His life has much more depth than ours—He is the Source of life!—but we, too, can tell people a little bit about what God has done or is doing in our lives, even in the middle of a much broader conversation.

6. Stop telling your story when it leads into other people telling theirs. It is pretty clear that Jesus shifted gears here and followed her into her own life. He had given her some pretty important things to think about. Now He wanted to help her see how it connected with her reality.

7. Enter into their story. Somehow Jesus was "safe" enough for her to allow Him into her story. She knew that He knew things about her and that He wasn't handling that knowledge the way that other religious people often did. He was still there, He wasn't judging her, and He didn't seem fazed. In fact, He was drawing her out even more! He didn't listen and move on. He got involved.

8. Share truth, but don't be concerned if you can't get into the whole thing yet. There came a point when Jesus spoke directly to the Samaritan woman about Himself. He never was coy or elusive about it, but a direct testimony to the core elements of the gospel was preceded by all that dialogue and question-asking. Ultimately, people need the gospel more than your story, but communicating your story can be a critical tool to get them there.

This story, in one sense, is unique. Jesus is the Son of God,

and we can't ever be as good as He is. What I think these principles show, however, is that there is plenty we can learn from His example. He modeled a way of treating people that we can follow.

How do I start?

As the wheels start to turn for you on being able to tell your story, here are some practical suggestions. These "warm-up" activities will help you to have the ability to engage with others.

Know your own story

When I was first learning to share my own story, I found it very helpful to grab a pen and my journal and write out my answers to the following questions. (By the way, if you don't journal, it is a good time to start!)

> What has God done in my life?
> What did He save me from?
> How did He do it?
> Whom did He use to help me understand what it is all about?
> When did this happen, and/or when did it start?
> Where did it happen or start to happen?
> How has He continued to change me?

By answering these questions for yourself, a few things might happen. First, you might be surprised and encouraged at just how powerful His hand has been in your life. Second, you might also begin to see that your story is not boring at all! Finally, by writing it down, you will begin to develop a vocabulary with which to describe your personal experience with Jesus.

Having some ability to name real names, times, places, and things that changed in you will help you learn how to share your story as opportunities arise.

Ask others to tell you their story

When I was just getting started, I found it helpful to ask believing friends what their stories were. It was helpful on a few levels. It helped me to correlate my story with theirs and gave a level of validation to my own story; it gave me some practice in drawing people out on their stories; and, finally, it was amazing how it drew us together.

This same exercise is just as important with non-believing friends. Making a concerted effort to ask my friends who do not yet know Christ what their story is has taught me many things. As I listen to my friends, I learn language for talking about God that isn't "churchy" and that I can apply to my own story. These stories almost always open up new avenues that help me relate to my friends on a deeper level. They also naturally generate opportunities to communicate my story with them, not because I have set them up but because I have given the conversation a nudge toward things that are a little deeper. If someone has to take a day off work to go to their grandmother's funeral, it would likely be natural to ask them what they thought about funerals. It could also lead to a question about what kind of faith they grew up with and, eventually, to a much longer story about where they currently are in their faith. You never know how God might open doors for conversation.

Learning to ask good questions and recognize what questions are okay to ask is a vital skill and can only be developed with practice. Of course, when you ask a question, it is essential that you listen well to the answer, for it will often lead to another question!

Abandon small agendas

As you prepare to talk with friends, it is important to think about why. Your top agenda in developing your story is not to convert your friends. Your top agenda is to bring glory to our King by appropriately highlighting the "precious diamond"—your story—that God has given you. Remember, as His child, your story ultimately showcases His story. By telling your story, you are telling His.

Like an engaged woman who proudly wears her ring (and loves to show it to others!), we are to wear, with dignity and appropriate pride, the story God has given us. It is beautiful, and it is worth showing.

Our agenda is an important issue to settle with God. Develop your story with all your heart, but do it for the glory of God. The agenda of bearing His name is enough.

Be with people . . . often

The more time we are with people, the more opportunities there will be for us to share our story. If we find ourselves in real life with real people, real moments will emerge.

For those of us with a strong Christian heritage, getting time with people can often mean tough decisions about who we're with and how often. If you don't have any (or very many) nonbelieving friends, that is something that likely needs to change. You might need to make some difficult choices about your schedule and priorities.

Pray

If you ask the Lord to help you identify and articulate your story, I believe that He will do it. Remember, your story is a contributing source to His story. He wants people to know His story—and He gave you yours—so, of course, He will help you to develop it, gain vocabulary for it, and provide opportunity to engage with others about it.

Get to work!

Let's consider again what Jesus modeled for us in John 4. Here is a review of the eight principles we explored earlier and a few practical suggestions as you move into engaging with others.

1. **Live your life.** Trust God for and pray for opportunities in the natural pathways of your life. We usually just need to have our eyes opened to what is already there.

2. **Go out of your way to treat others with dignity.** Small efforts here stand out. A word here, a good deed there. As we engage in living this way, opportunities will abound.

3. **Be alert for opportunities to go deeper with them.** I have found that opportunities show up at surprising times and in surprising ways. We need to be alert and ready so that we can step into them.

4. **Listen well.** There is a shortage of people who listen well. Stand out in this world by being someone who listens first.

5. **Share your story, but leave room for conversation.** The most likely scenario here is that you are talking with a friend. Talking with a friend involves give-and-take. Learn to share your story in this way.

6. **Stop telling your story when it leads into other people telling theirs.** As your friend starts to talk about himself, be ready to stop talking about yourself.

7. **Enter into their story.** Sometimes it will be obvious that it is okay to really draw people out about their story. Other time, it will be harder to tell, a bit more mysterious. But as you take small risks and people open the door, do not neglect to go in.

8. **Share truth, but don't be concerned if you can't get into the whole thing yet.** It can be easy to think that people

need to hear everything in one sitting—but this is just not true. Remember that Jesus is what they need more than your story. Be ready to tell your story, but also be ready for it to take some time.

Final Thought

You have a precious diamond that no one else has. It is part of the great treasure that our King has. You are one of His treasures. Your story of His work in your life is brilliant, powerful, and priceless.

May you become all that He intended by letting others see it. And may many be swept up into His story through yours.

9

READING THE BIBLE WITH FRIENDS WHO DON'T BELIEVE IT

Jim Petersen

Jim Petersen and his late wife, Marge, worked as a team with The Navigators since 1958 and pioneered the work of the ministry in Brazil. Jim is now an associate to the general director. "Reading the Bible with Friends Who Don't Believe It" was first published in 2013.

WHAT DO YOU WANT OUT OF LIFE? Almost everyone approaches life with high expectations. We want our lives to count for something.

We enter the workforce. It's a shock. The job turns out to be far more demanding than we ever imagined. Responsibilities pile up, and the boss doesn't feel sorry for us. Soon the many demands of life and the surrounding cacophony of voices that tell us, sell us, beg and cajole us distract us from our aspirations. Life compounds in complexity. A decade sneaks by, and now we believe that it's too late to accomplish anything meaningful. So we coast along, with our regrets growing deeper and deeper by the year.

As you know, this is the story for a lot of people. You ask, "What are my chances of doing any better?" I'll let you answer the question for yourself as you work your way through this essay. I think you will be greatly encouraged.

First, we need to settle on what, indeed, is significant. For that we need a map big enough to find our way across life. There is only one such map. It is the Bible. True significance is found as we align ourselves with God's purposes and engage with Him in what He's doing in the world. So our question is: What is He up to?

You don't have to read the entire Bible to get your answer. He has done us the favor of providing us with His mission statement in just a few words. Here it is.

> For he chose us in him before the creation of the world
> . . . to be adopted as his sons through Jesus Christ. . . .
> In him we have redemption through his blood, the
> forgiveness of sins. . . . And he made known to us the
> mystery of his will . . . which he purposed in Christ
> . . . to bring all things in heaven and on earth together
> under one head, even Christ.
> EPHESIANS 1:4-5, 7, 9-10, NIV

What do you think? Notice that this plan is dated from "before the creation of the world," and it remains in force until the whole universe is healed and established under Christ's kingship. Did you observe what's at the center of it? It's *people*. He is redeeming people, but it's at an awful cost. It cost Him the *cross* for His son. Through that death, He is creating an eternal family, people who are "fellow citizens . . . members of God's household" (Ephesians 2:19, NIV).

God is invested in people. This is at the heart of everything He is doing. And the most amazing thing about this enterprise is that He has chosen to partner with us.

> God was reconciling the world to himself in Christ.
> . . . And he has committed to us the message of reconciliation.
>
> 2 CORINTHIANS 5:19, NIV

He has invited us to join Him! To act on that invitation is to experience what is truly significant. As you read this, you might be thinking, *I chose the wrong career. I work behind a computer all day.*

Don't listen to that voice. You already have a lot more going for you than you imagine when it comes to participating with God in His work. I have had the opportunity to devote my life to just this enterprise. With this privilege comes the responsibility to pass on what I have learned along the way and to, hopefully, save you some time and frustration as you pursue your calling. So here's a bit of my story. Watch for the principles, not just the methods. Methods will vary with each situation.

Just Show Them "The Bridge"

A little more than a half century ago, in 1955, I was a student at the University of Minnesota, newly married and working a part-time job. Previously, I had toyed with existentialism, and to settle my doubts I had read the four Gospels of the New Testament to see for myself who that man, Jesus, really was. He had claimed to be God. For me, if that story held up under scrutiny, my questions would be answered. That story not only held up—it took over. It left me with an insatiable desire to learn all I could about Him. I soon realized that I needed outside help, so I turned to a person who obviously knew a lot more about it than I did. His name was Ed Reis. Ed mentored and taught me. At that time, the magical words for me were "how to." I wanted practical stuff, tools I could use to make my own discoveries in the Bible and understand it in such a way that it would be transformational to my life. Then I found that the more I learned, the more I longed to pass it on.

One day, Ed showed me an illustration called "The Bridge." It was exactly what I had been looking for, a succinct explanation of the gospel. For me, evangelism consisted of explaining the gospel to someone and then calling for the vote. I had been praying for a number of my classmates at the University of Minnesota and now, with this illustration in hand, I was eager to show it to these friends.

Lunchtimes were perfect. Many students would come to school with a sandwich in their book bag. They would eat it at lunchtime in one of the student lounges. That's what I did, and so did my friends. I decided that I would approach each of them and say something like, "Hey, let's have lunch together today. I have something I want to show you." "Sure!" they'd answer. It was natural. Over the following weeks I made the rounds, one by one.

We would sit down at a table together, and I would pull out a piece of paper and get started. As we got into it, I would take a New Testament out of my book bag, and we would discuss our way through the illustration, verse by verse. At a certain point, I would ask, "Where are you in this picture, on the 'death' or on the 'life' side?" Then I'd ask him which he was choosing. I was amazed and excited as several friends responded positively and started a new life in Christ.

Fast-forward eight years, to 1964. My wife, Marge, and I, together with our two young children, found ourselves living in the city of Curitiba, a provincial capital of one of the south-central states in Brazil. We had chosen that city as the place to begin a Navigators ministry in the country. We were starting from scratch—didn't know a single person in town. I had just one lead: a name, Osvaldo, and corresponding phone number written on a scrap of paper. I tracked him down and invited him to our house for dinner.

Osvaldo was really curious. What was an American couple with two very small children doing in a city like Curitiba? As we ate our dinner around the table, he plied us with questions, intent on getting an answer that made sense to him. I was cautious, evasive. After all, he was the only contact we had in the entire city. I didn't want to scare him off. He insisted. We verbally danced around until dinner was over. Then I picked up a piece of chalk, grabbed my Portuguese Bible, found an open

spot on the polished wood floor, and squatted down. I invited
Osvaldo to do the same.

The hardwood floor served as my chalkboard. I explained
to him that I had an illustration that would answer his question about our move to Brazil. It was "The Bridge." We spent
the next hour and a half drawing lines on the floor and looking
up verses in the Bible. I'd find the verse, turn my Bible around,
and ask him to read it. Then I'd ask him what he thought it
said. We'd work at a verse until it was clear to him. In that way,
Osvaldo was explaining the Bible to himself.

As we wound down, I was feeling good. I knew we had communicated with each other. So I leaned back, folded my arms,
and asked him where he was in the picture we had composed.
I was stunned at his response. He looked at our work, looked
back at me, then at the work again, shook his head, and said,
"I don't get it. You mean you came all the way to Brazil to show
people *that*?" He was totally puzzled.

As he responded in that way, something Jesus once said to
His disciples flashed into my mind.

> I sent you to reap what you have not worked for.
> Others have done the hard work, and you have reaped
> the benefits of their labor.
> JOHN 4:38, NIV

Jesus was preparing His disciples to take the gospel to their
fellow Jews, a people who had the benefit of twenty centuries

of sowing and cultivating. People like Abraham, Isaac, Jacob, Moses, David, Isaiah, Daniel, and more recently, John the Baptist made up their heritage. It was harvest time among the Jews, and Jesus was getting His disciples ready for it. The "hard work" of planting and cultivating had already been done for them over those centuries. And here was Osvaldo, showing no apparent signs of any previous labor. What was I to do?

Think Like a Farmer

That comment by Jesus on reaping was very instructive for me. It's farmer talk. He often used that same farming metaphor to describe the process God employs in drawing people to Himself.[1] When a person moves from unbelief to faith in Christ, it is always a process, not just an event. It takes planting and cultivating before there can be reaping. Few people are readily "reap-able," but many, many more are reachable—if we are patient.

I asked Osvaldo if he would like to get together again to read and talk more. He said he would. It became a pattern. Over the next three months he would come to our house a couple times a week. He would join our family at the supper table, and then the two of us would get our Bibles out and go at it. We went to John's Gospel and conversed our way through it. Our primary question was, "Who was Jesus?" Those were months of struggle for Osvaldo, but there came a point when faith trumped doubt, and he joined God's family. He ended up spending the next three years living with us, and what a fruitful life he has lived since then!

As for me, I was on a steep learning curve. Everything I thought I knew how to do was being challenged by the new realities we were dealing with. Fortunately, in response to the challenges, the Lord was consistently bringing Scriptures to mind that would instruct me in what to do next. Mark 4:26-29 was one passage that profoundly influenced what we did:

> This is what the kingdom of God is like. A man
> scatters seed on the ground. Night and day, whether he
> sleeps or gets up, the seed sprouts and grows, though
> he does not know how. All by itself the soil produces
> grain—first the stalk, then the head, then the full
> kernel in the head. As soon as the grain is ripe, he
> puts the sickle to it, because the harvest has come.
> MARK 4:26-29

This little story gives us a good description of the dynamics of the process. We are the farmers in this story. We're clueless, but we do what we know to do. We sow. Then God does the rest. What a relief that is!

On another occasion, Jesus told almost the same story, but this time He explained, "The one who sowed the good seed is the Son of Man" (Matthew 13:37, NIV). Here, in this telling of the story, God is the farmer, not us.

Well, which is it? Who does the sowing, God or us? The

answer is—yes! In this second narration *we* are the good seed, not the sower! To quote Jesus, "The field is the world, and the good seed stands for the sons of the kingdom" (Matthew 13:38, NIV).

Confused? Good! Where do we draw the line between God's part and ours in kingdom business? We can't. Didn't Jesus tell us, "Apart from me you can do nothing" (John 15:5, NIV)? We are profoundly dependent on Him.

On Being Salt, Light, and Seed

Jesus used a variety of metaphors to describe our part in His workings. He called us "the salt of the earth" and "the light of the world" (Matthew 5:13-14, NIV) and said that we are "good seed" (Matthew 13:38, NIV). What do these things have in common? With each, a little bit can go a long way. A few grains of salt on a plate of food, a candle in a dark room, or a handful of seeds in a garden—each has the power to transform, and each accomplishes its purpose by being scattered into its immediate environment.

Light was one of Jesus' favorite metaphors. On one occasion He said, "I have come into the world as a light, so that no one who believes in me should stay in darkness" (John 12:46, NIV). In another place He extended that function to us. He said, "You are the light of the world. . . . Let your light shine before men, that they may see your good deeds and praise your Father in heaven" (Matthew 5:14, 16, NIV).

The apostle Paul picked up on this metaphor. In his letter to the Ephesians, he wrote, "For you were once darkness, but now you are light in the Lord. Live as children of light" (Ephesians 5:8, NIV). Why is this important? It's because we are surrounded by people who are asleep in the dark. Paul went on to say,

This is why it is said:

"Wake up, O sleeper,
    rise from the dead,
and Christ will shine on you."
EPHESIANS 5:14, NIV

Who's the sleeper here? It's somebody who is not only asleep but dead! It's the way that Paul's readers in Ephesus were before they received the gospel. Earlier in the letter, he wrote, "As for you, you were dead in your transgressions and sins" (Ephesians 2:1, NIV). You will need to go soak yourself in the book of Ephesians to get the context and the full impact of what he's saying here. It will be worth your effort. But the bottom line is that God intends for us to live in such a way that we are like a spotlight shining into the eyes of a person who is in a dead sleep.

This awakening was what was happening with Osvaldo, but I was oblivious to it at the time. The hours that we spent in the Scriptures were significant, but the real eye-opener came during those mealtimes with our family. He saw a family living in the light. He wanted that for himself. It took a long time for me to grasp this, to understand that it is as much what people see as it is what they hear that intrigues and attracts them to Christ.

I met Mario at a lecture on educational theory at the University of Parana. I was interpreting for the lecturer, who was from Switzerland. Mario took issue with some things the lecturer said, so he came to the podium afterward to talk with us. After a bit of vigorous discussion, I suggested that if he wanted to talk further, we could meet in my office just down the street. He did, and we did.

At the time, Mario was a dental student at the university, an intellectual with Marxist leanings who was also active in political protests against the Brazilian government. He had never considered the Scriptures before, but he was intrigued by what I was showing him. They were provocative; they made him think. We met once or twice a week, off and on, for four years, before he was ready to let Christ rule. In the course of our conversations we became real friends. We hiked, did some mountain climbing, and had a lot of meals together, some at my home.

One day, a couple years after he had put his faith in Christ, we were reminiscing. Mario asked me, "What do you think it was that persuaded me to follow Christ?" In my mind, I thought about the thousand hours of Bible study we had done. But he said, "I watched the way you and Marge related to each other and what went on between you and your children, and I asked myself, *Mario, when will you have a family like this?* I had to admit that it would be never! So I had to choose Christ for the sake of my own survival."

Over the years, Marge and I have gotten similar feedback from many friends like Mario. All the stories have one thing in common. People were attracted and then convinced of the truth of the gospel as much by the little things they experienced in the course of our friendship as they were by the Scriptures. It was the love, the caring, the hospitality, and the serving (usually at the hands of my wife) that validated the message.

The point is that if you are pursuing Christ *and letting people who need Him into your life*, you *are* sowing the gospel. You *are* being good seed and are probably already further down the road than you imagined in bearing fruit in God's enterprise.

Supernatural Resources

In yet another telling of the parable of the sower, Jesus added one more nuance. This time He explained that "the seed is the word of God" (Luke 8:11, NIV). That makes sense. The Scriptures need to be part of the dynamic in our interaction with our friends. When that happens, a whole new dimension opens up. That's because . . .

> The word of God is living and active. Sharper than any double-edged sword, it penetrates even to dividing soul and spirit, joints and marrow; it judges the thoughts and attitudes of the heart.
>
> HEBREWS 4:12, NIV

If you have been around the Scriptures at all, you know from experience what this means. There you are, reading along, and—*wham!* Something stops you—an insight, an assurance, or a warning, as if God was reading your mind. He *is* reading your mind—and your heart and your soul! In the hands of the Holy Spirit, the Book comes alive.

This can also happen to a person who doesn't believe the Bible. It's still the "sword of the Spirit" (Ephesians 6:17, NIV) and can still pierce that person to the core. So use it. This gives the Holy Spirit powerful leverage. In the middle of the night, on a morning jog, the Holy Spirit will bring something from the Scriptures to that person's mind. Thus the seed germinates.

As we continue to participate in this process, we intercede for our friends. What are we to ask for? Jesus, as He described the coming of the Holy Spirit to His disciples, explained it like this:

> When he comes, he will convict the world of guilt in regard to sin and righteousness and judgment.
> JOHN 16:8, NIV

I've found this to be a good guide. I ask God to help my friends see their *sin* for what it is and to understand that they don't measure up to God's *righteousness* and therefore will face God's *judgment*.

In the early days, I thought it was my job to convince people of these things, and as a result I created some really awkward moments. What a relief it is to be able to leave this part to the Holy Spirit! Now I watch, pray, sympathize with my friend as he or she struggles, and keep on sowing until the seed takes root. I'm along for the ride.

The Big Question

The most frequent question that most of us struggle with at this point is: How do I get beyond football, fashion, or all the other small talk and really engage in the subject of knowing God with a friend? It's one thing to engage in a discussion after a lecture, but how can I include God in a normal conversation?

Frequently, I, too, struggle with this, but I've learned something. I have discovered that the more my friend and I know about each other, the easier such conversations become. It looks like this: You tell me your story, I'll tell you my story, and that will take us to God's story.

Robert and I have been acquaintances for twenty years. Recently, some business matters increased our involvement with each other. In the course of things, he and I, together with our wives, needed to travel to another city. While on the two-hour trip, we got them to tell their story.

Since then, Robert and I have made it a point to get together every week or two for lunch. I have given him my story in bits and pieces. Because my story is incomplete if I don't include the things that influenced me to pursue a relationship with God, that has been part of our conversations. As both stories have come out, our mutual trust has grown, and a larger context for further conversations has been created. Now we both know where the other is coming from and what to expect from the other. Robert has become accustomed to me weaving biblical ideas into our conversations, even though God still seems to be absent from his worldview.

As of this writing, Robert's story is unfinished. At my suggestion, he has taken a copy of *The Message* with him on vacation. His intention is to read the four Gospels to see for himself what Jesus was all about. Of course, I'm praying that Jesus will come off those pages for him as he reads!

Teaming Up!

You will need help if you are to succeed at what we're talking about. You will need a core group of kindred spirits who share your vision and can encourage you. For me, that core group has been my wife and a few other like-minded people, including our children. It is so easy to procrastinate, to wait for someone or some program to come along that you can join that will help you fulfill your aspirations. But you could die waiting. It's your move!

Teaming up can get you there. Why do you suppose, when Jesus sent the seventy-two out to the various villages to set things up for His visits, He had them go in pairs? Or why did the apostle Paul always team up with another, such as Barnabas or Silas? Solomon answered this question for us:

Two are better than one,
    because they have a good return for their work:
If one falls down,
    his friend can help him up.
But pity the man who falls,
    and has no one to help him up! . . .
Though one may be overpowered,
    two can defend themselves.
A cord of three strands is not quickly broken.
ECCLESIASTES 4:9-10, 12, NIV

As we team up, our strengths are compounded and our weaknesses are moderated. We are part of a body, made up of many interdependent parts. Everybody is good at something, but no one is good at everything. Together we can accomplish what would otherwise be beyond our reach individually.

Reading the Bible with Your Friends

Often, individual friendships, such as the ones I have been describing, can become the foundation of a small group of people that have a certain affinity with each other. Given the right setting, many people would be eager to engage in Bible-based discussions.

My friend Jeff did something like that with some of his business associates. He used a Bible study series that explores the meaning of work.[2] (Who doesn't want to know what that period of sixty hours a week is all about?!) He chose to use the boardroom in his office as their venue. They met on Friday mornings before work. He made a list of ten people and began to pray for each of them. Then, one by one, he invited them. When the first nine said yes, Jeff thought, *This is too easy.* His tenth person, however, was the guy he considered least likely to accept. Much to Jeff's surprise, he also said yes.

What's the draw? Many people struggle with doubt over their own notions of life and truth. They know they haven't really done their homework, and when an opportunity comes along to do some cross-checking, especially with a few people they already know, they'll take it. Safe places, where there are no strings attached, are rare. The Bible might still be a remote book to them, but under the right conditions they're willing to see what it has to say.

Try it! Find a running mate. Then, together, prayerfully make a list of people in your lives who you think would fit with each other. Then go talk to them. Your knees might knock a bit, but do it. Your invitation needs to be relevant, something like, "We have been thinking about getting a few friends together to read the Bible. We find that we need its wisdom to help us keep our heads screwed on straight. You're our friend, so we're inviting you. I'll let you know when we're ready to go."

Notice how, in this invitation, you are recognizing that you, too, need what this group promises and that you're expecting there to be mutual benefit. Give your friends some time and space to digest the idea. Then just put it together.

At this point, you might be thinking, *Who am I to say anything to anybody? My friends know too much about me. You know—the tacky stuff.* Don't let your personal weaknesses silence you. Instead, let them lead you to the greatest lesson of all. As the apostle Paul put it, "I will boast all the more gladly about my weaknesses, so that Christ's power may rest on me. That is why, for Christ's sake, I delight in weaknesses. . . . For when I am weak, then I am strong" (2 Corinthians 12:9-10, NIV). When you recognize your weaknesses, you also know how dependent you are.

You're not perfect, and you never will be. Accept that. Don't try to fake it. Be vulnerable, and trust God to make up the difference. You will see Him act, treating you with grace and making things happen that are beyond you. The experience will greatly enhance your walk with Christ.

Tips for Getting Started

1. **Set the atmosphere.** Choose a comfortable, normal meeting place, like in a home or an office. Songs, prayers, and religious language don't fit here. There will come a time when prayer will become an important part of things, but don't start there. If you decide to meet in a home, rotate between homes.

2. **Small is beautiful.** Participants can number from two to ten, twelve at the most. If it gets bigger than that, true discussion becomes difficult. Someone ends up preaching, and it becomes a class, not a discussion.

3. **Timing.** Don't be late, and don't go over time. Stop talking before people stop listening. The schedule has to be predictable so that people can plan accordingly.

4. **Stick with the Bible** even if people are unfamiliar with it. Explain that there are two parts to the Bible, the Old Testament and the New Testament, that the big numbers are chapters and that the little numbers are called verses, and so on. Don't assume that people have any prior knowledge of it.

5. **Subject matter.** There are several good options as starting points, such as the meaning of work, child-rearing, or whatever constitutes an open nerve for your friends. But all roads eventually lead to the single question: Who was Jesus? Help people get a fresh look at Him. When they do, they will embrace Him.

6. **Prepare for a session** with questions that help probe the text. Keep the sessions interactive. Encourage people to read ahead, but don't expect much preparation on their part. Create an environment in which questions can flourish. Everyone will be wondering, "Is it safe to ask my real questions around here?" Make sure it is.

Tips for Keeping the Group Vital

1. **Touch base with each person during the week**, whether personally, via e-mail, or by phone.

2. **Keep the discussion moving** and on track. Keep rabbit trails to a minimum. Keep hospitality simple so that the event doesn't become an ordeal for the host.

3. **Spiritual births.** Be patient. A true conversion involves the emotions, the intellect, and the will. A mere emotional response doesn't last. The intellect needs to be satisfied that this step to faith stands up to reason. But the real struggle is with the will. It asks, "Am I willing to submit myself to Christ?" It takes time for most people to honestly wrestle with this decision. Many spiritual births will occur unassisted, as people ponder what they are receiving from the Scriptures. Sometimes a person needs a little help. That's where "The Bridge" can be very useful. True spiritual birth is obvious and robust.

4. **Life span of a group.** How long should a particular group remain intact? Since the goal goes beyond spiritual birth to maturity, you can expect to spend three or four years with a particular group. In that time, you will become the best of friends, and it will be difficult to separate. But the time will come when you'll need to reconfigure the group to accommodate others, those who have been attracted by what they have observed in their friends.

5. **Generations.** Each person in the group has family and friends. Concerns for them will surface as familiarity

grows within the group. Agree to pray for these people. When the time comes to reconfigure the group, divide up and invite those people you have been praying for to participate. You should never run out of opportunities.

True Significance

What do you think? What could be more significant than participating with God as He transforms people's lives—moving your friends and family from futility to hope, from pain to joy, and from conflict to love? God's truth heals. The apostle John said it best: "I have no greater joy than to hear that my children are walking in the truth" (3 John 4, NIV).

I have lived long enough to witness the power of generational growth. It seems slow in the beginning, but the growth is exponential. Ron was a college kid when he began his walk with Christ. He married, and the two have walked with Him together. Then they guided their children accordingly. They are grandparents now, and I counted seventeen people in their last family photo. There is, of course, no guarantee that all will follow Christ, but their heritage gives them every advantage. They have also been contagious among their friends, several of whom are now on the same trajectory. Ron and his family are salt, light, and good seed. With no bells or whistles, they have enriched the people around them and transformed their destinies.

The least of you will become a thousand,
    the smallest a mighty nation.
I am the LORD;
    in its time I will do this swiftly.
ISAIAH 60:22, NIV

This promise is for you!

HOW DO WE CREATE A LIFE-GIVING ATMOSPHERE?

Dana Yeakley

Dana Yeakley and her husband, Tom, have been serving with The Navigators since 1978. Having been involved in a collegiate couple's ministry at Purdue University from 1973 to 1981, they worked in church discipleship ministries in the greater Chicago area and then moved to Indonesia to serve in collegiate and community ministries there before returning to the United States. Dana has served as an associate director on The Navigators Collegiate Leadership Team, as a trainer, account executive, and center director for LearningRX, and on the national leadership team for Navigators 20s ministry. The following comes from her 2016 book, The Gentle Art of Discipling Women.

But we were gentle among you, like a nursing mother taking care of her own children. So, being affectionately desirous of you, we were ready to share with you not only the gospel of God but also our own selves, because you had become very dear to us.

I THESSALONIANS 2:7-8, ESV

MY LONGTIME FRIEND, Cindy, lives in Chicago. I've always loved going to her house because it fills me with a sense of coming home. She has created an environment of relational warmth, comfort, and love. I feel safe there. And I am certain that many others have enjoyed her ability to create an atmosphere that draws people in and invites them to connect from the heart.

Healthy discipling relationships require a similar atmosphere. Like Cindy, whose home draws people to feel accepted and loved, we want to ensure a relational setting that will help those we disciple feel safe and cared for. None of us are just alike in how we disciple or in the atmosphere we offer and relate in. This is because all of us operate from the person God created us to be. We all have talents, skills, personality traits, relational strengths, and a desire to love. So let's think through and own the atmosphere that will flow from who each of us are and how God has wired us individually as we disciple others! Owning the atmosphere we offer will facilitate enjoyment, satisfaction, and growth for us and those we help.

Perspective Check

Before we answer the question of how we create the right atmosphere, we must consider two key perspectives that inform the environment. These perspectives, which we see Jesus modeling in Matthew 9, can be boiled down to two questions: Do we see people, and are we willing to get involved with them?

Do We See People?

We will undergo a vision shift as we take on Jesus' heart for discipling. As our perspective matures, we begin to "see" people like He does. In Matthew 9:36-38, we are given a glimpse of Jesus' heart as He sees the massive throng surrounding Him:

> *Seeing* the crowds, He felt compassion for them, because they were distressed and downcast, like sheep without a shepherd. Then He said to His disciples, "The harvest is plentiful, but the workers are few. Therefore, plead with the Lord of the harvest to send out workers into His harvest."
>
> NASB (EMPHASIS ADDED)

Imagine yourself standing among the disciples at this moment. Do you see what a compassionate Savior Jesus is? Jesus directly connects the distressed and dispirited sheep before us to the great harvest of souls for which He came. What good is it to meet any other need if the greatest need is not met? As we begin to see people like Jesus sees people, we can then take part in the great adventure of laboring with Him. "Seeing" people like Jesus sees them is our ground zero as we step into discipling.

Recently my daughter, Amy, sent me these words after her morning walk around her neighborhood:

> *Look at me*
> *See me*
> *Listen to me*
> *Hear me*

Eyes peeking through patterned and tattered head scarf
Lips tight with wrinkles defining the years
Hands folded while briskly walking
Mismatched skirt loosely wrapped around a thin waist
Feet moving in worn-out sandals
seeking an unknown destination
Look at me
See me
Listen to me
Hear me
Dark twinkling eyes
Braided hair complete with colored clips
bouncing while trying to stand still
A smile from ear to ear
Backpack held with firm and confident hands
Joyful, spirited, and eager for all the school day holds
Look at me
See me
Listen to me
Hear me
Clinging in fear of the buzzing bee
Jacket askew
Begging for anyone to protect from the ferocious stinger
Sweaty palms
Anxiety and distress
Look at me
See me

Listen to me
Hear me
Head down
Hands stuffed in pockets
Alone
When greeted, posture changed and a light turned on
Look at me
See me
Listen to me
Hear me[1]

I love how Amy articulated the need each person had to be seen and heard as she crossed paths with them. How about you? Do you "see" people? Before we can create an atmosphere that will serve those we disciple, we need to see people as Jesus sees them, in the midst of a broken and harrowing world.

Will We Get Involved with People?

We might be busy with a variety of activities, but if we want to share in the heart of Jesus, we must relate to and invest in people like Jesus did.

This shift began to occur in my heart in 1975. I was involved in discipleship studies at Purdue University, and one night I attended a prayer focus with a small group of women. Our prayer guide had us pray over Matthew 9:36-38. I do not recall praying anything out loud. What I do recall is that as the prayers of others echoed around me, God began speaking to me in a quiet but commanding voice, asking me if I was willing to be one of those workers Jesus was talking about in Matthew 9.

My inner spirit trembled at the Holy Spirit's question. I was reluctant to surrender because I was aware of many stories that described how God was sending out workers around the world. I was not sure of what this would mean for my family. Honestly, I was concerned that I would have to leave home and serve overseas. But that night, I relinquished my future quietly to His voice and over the next few years committed to learning about what it means to labor in His harvest.

Although a major shift started in my heart during that prayer time, there was no instant change. God showed me and Tom the imperative need for our own personal growth and training before we could step out as laborers. And after it was all said and done, God did ask our family to go overseas. Serving overseas was undeniably difficult but absolutely fulfilling—because it was what God asked us to do.

Jesus engaged in many activities: miraculous healings, driving out demons, turning water into wine, debating with the Jewish leaders, having personal conversations with the lost, and even raising the dead! Imagine His popularity among the people as they realized His power. In Mark we find the disciples looking for Him because the crowds wanted Him to continue doing the amazing things He had done the night before. But listen to what Jesus says as He clarifies why He came:

When they found him, they exclaimed: "Everyone is looking for you!"

Jesus replied, "Let us go somewhere else—to the nearby villages—so I can preach there also. That is why I have come."

MARK 1:37-38, NIV

Jesus brought the good news and was committed to preaching His eternal message—and to do it, He got involved with the people around Him. By healing and helping many as He walked among people, Jesus gained a following. During His brief ministry on earth, many people began to realize who He really was and why He came.

Jesus modeled for us what it meant to be involved with people. His purposeful investment in the disciples was foundational to meeting the needs of the world. He preached the Kingdom, knowing that His disciples would take what He taught to the nations after He was gone.

Creating an Atmosphere

A friend of mine always welcomes those she disciples into her living room. On her coffee table sits a candle and a beautiful tea service with delicate refreshments. This is how she communicates value to the women she meets with. It flows from her personal talents and heart. When she engages with women, she is truly a life-giver.

When I meet with women, the environment I cultivate doesn't look like my friend's. I am not like her—and that's okay! While the ambiance that I offer flows from my heart as well, I have met with women in restaurants, coffee shops, and office settings. I even met with someone in a rather plush bathroom at a high-end Nordstrom once! In the past few years, I have really focused on inviting women into my home. Or—especially if they have little children—I go to their home. The home is a place where we are in charge of the noise and have opportunities to share deeply and pray inconspicuously.

Though location and physical setting are important, they are merely the concrete aspects within which the atmosphere flows. The key atmosphere choices we make are intangible yet crucial. Every discipleship relationship should include five specific ingredients that will help ensure a life-giving atmosphere.

1. Confidentiality

Confidentiality means that we offer strict privacy for all that we share in conversation and life with someone. Confidentiality creates a safe environment. Now, some of us find a commitment to confidentiality easier than others do. I have been around women who have shared prayer requests that reveal the weaknesses of another woman. A friend once asked me to pray for someone who had shared something with her confidentially. We must not do this. Confidentiality is a privilege we carry. We have been entrusted with a precious piece of someone's heart, and we need to beware of telling others about her needs without her permission.

Never should a need, a weakness, a concern, or a fear of someone we disciple become a prayer request that we share with someone else. There is a word for this when we do this: *gossip*!

Confidentiality creates trust and authentic exchange as we meet with those we disciple. When we fall short in this area, we need to quickly amend the broken trust.

2. Relationship

The atmosphere at the heart of our discipling relationships should lean heavily toward being relational. We must view ourselves as coming alongside a friend, seeking to develop a rapport that produces mutual fondness and trust. As a wise man once told me, "We must build the bridge of relationship strong enough to bear the weight of truth." We are not ahead of those we disciple, nor are we behind them. Relationship affords us the opportunity to stand next to someone as we guide them forward.

Seasons of life will color how we build relationships. In my earlier days, I would often plan a get-together or a fun activity with those I was discipling. Usually during this season of life, we were the same age or just a few years apart. We did things that we both enjoyed, from shopping to going to the playground with our kids. Sometimes we might take a day trip together or go to a concert or play.

How we build relationships may change as seasons of life

change. Other older women I know invite younger women over to cook or help in some home project. Some garden together. Others go on walks. While there are many ways to connect, I have found that when there is a vast age difference, we don't always have to "do something" to create trust and enjoyment in our relationship.

Another important piece of building relationships? Laughing together! Laughing together produces a natural path to openness. The discipling relationship has a way of touching our scary vulnerable spots. Being able to laugh together amid shared vulnerability creates an important emotional connection.

Emphasizing relationship is crucial for discipling. A genuine relationship frees us to share whatever we need to with the assurance of acceptance, care, and love.

3. *Affirmation*

Affirmation is not flattery. Flattery is defined as excessive or insincere praise. Flattery is a kind of inflated truth and can easily be manipulative. Compliments are also different from affirmation. Compliments tend to offer homage or applause to someone. That is okay. We do want to call out that which a person is good at. But compliments also can have a manipulative aspect and can be superfluous or even distracting from the deeper aspects of a person's heart and character.

Affirmation involves the assertion that something is true. Affirmation is a solid assessment offered to someone that speaks to character and growth. Affirmation speaks to what God is doing in and through a person. Listening to someone attentively as they share their heart affirms their value. We can affirm someone even as we pray for and bless them.

These questions can help us as we seek to affirm those we disciple:

> What is true and good about this woman?
> What is God doing "in her" that is wonderful?
> How is she responding in truth to Christ as He leads her down a difficult path?
> What aspect of her character that reflects kindness, godliness, or compassion might I commend?

Pay attention to her spiritual progress as you hear her share about her life. Asking good questions is an indispensable skill that invites those we disciple to analyze and investigate their responses and issues. Share your life experience when it is in sync with her experience or need, but for the most part let her do the talking. Listening to and hearing someone's heart is a form of affirmation. And we don't always have to have an answer. In fact, not having the answer is good because we can always pray with and for her. Trusting God alongside those we help models dependency on Him.

Including affirmation in our discipling atmosphere helps us to build another up, always offering grace and truth in the words we share.

4. *Intentionality*

Intentionality simply means that we engage in forethought and deliberate planning before acting. Jesus lived this way and taught this way with the twelve disciples over the three years He was in ministry (Mark 1:38). Even the word *disciple* contains the seeds for intentionality. A disciple is one who follows and learns. As we help someone follow Christ, we offer them opportunity for learning through prepared scriptural content.

To be intentional as we disciple merely means that we are responsibly thinking through what, how, and when we will share with those we meet with. It means that we offer structure with purpose for their growth. Have you ever attended a Zumba class where the instructor is not prepared? Without the intense continuous Latin movement, the hour seems slow and wasted. Just like I appreciate a well-planned total-dance workout from my Zumba instructor, so those we disciple deserve concerted attention to their growth needs.

Because I tend to be a more spontaneous person, I often struggle with the concepts of structuring time and planning content. It is so much easier for me to flow freely without preparation. I fall into this frequently, so I write this because I know this is what is best—even if I must work at it, even after years of discipling. Ultimately, I do the work of preparation because it is best for those I am discipling (not because I get a kick out of it!).

5. Love

True love in a healthy discipleship relationship has a couple different facets. First of all, love often includes exhortation. We live in an age where "love" is excessively tolerant. We are wary of saying anything that would deflate someone's self-image. When Jesus expressed love, He always spoke that which was most constructive for that person in the long run. He seemed to refrain from saying anything that would give someone a false sense of security (Mark 10:21). God is committed to the truth—*about us* and *for us*—because He loves us!

Exhortation is not only a spiritual gift but also a requirement for all believers (Hebrews 10:25). *Exhortation* means to convey urgent advice or recommendations. It is a combination of counsel and warning combined with a sense of caution. There is also a place for rebuke, should there be a need. Rebuke is stronger than exhortation and involves a stern talk or reprimand.

When I was in my twenties, the woman who discipled me told me that she was praying a certain verse over my life. The essence of this verse? That God would grow me from being a depressed personality to one who delights in Him. Her exhortation, though necessary and helpful, was hard to hear—but I paid attention. Indeed, I was often depressed, and my depression tended to "hang over" my life and conversations with others. Our brief conversation about that verse and her continued supportive prayer set me on a path of transformation and trust that changed me forever!

We need to be sensitive as we observe weaknesses in those we are helping. When we determine that we need to share something, we would be wise to first ask permission, regardless of a past agreement. And when we do take it upon ourselves to lovingly exhort or rebuke, we can purpose to avoid being blunt, abrasive, or condescending. We can bring truth with grace when we are sure that our exhortation will bring growth and eventually joy.

The second facet of love is that it needs to be unconditional. Unconditional love is absolute, total, and genuine. Because we are completely accepted by God, we must willingly accept others. Many broken people around us fear rejection. When we seek to truly love those around us, they need to know that there is nothing that they can do or say that will cause us to reject them. Communicating this kind of love creates an atmosphere that is safe and energized for mutual sharing.

When we love unconditionally, we are not saying we applaud or agree with sinful or selfish behavior. But we are saying that no matter what, we have their back!

※

If I was going to choose a passage that summarizes the atmosphere I long to create for the women I meet with, it would be Romans 12:9-18. As you read this passage, underline words that speak to your heart about creating the "right" atmosphere for discipling:

Love must be honest and true. Hate what is evil. Hold on to what is good. Love one another deeply. Honor others more than yourselves. Stay excited about your faith as you serve the Lord. When you hope, be joyful. When you suffer, be patient. When you pray, be faithful. Share with the Lord's people who are in need. Welcome others into your homes.

Bless those who hurt you. Bless them, and do not curse them. Be joyful with those who are joyful. Be sad with those who are sad. Agree with one another. Don't be proud. Be willing to be a friend of people who aren't considered important. Don't think that you are better than others.

Don't pay back evil with evil. Be careful to do what everyone thinks is right. If possible, live in peace with everyone. Do that as much as you can.

NIRV

11

BORN TO REPRODUCE

Dawson Trotman

Dawson Trotman, converted at age twenty, gave thirty years to vigorous pursuit of the goal "to know Christ and make Him known." Trotman was a man who believed God, who asked Him for great things and saw God answer. The ministry of The Navigators, which Trotman founded in 1933, is one of those answers. He led the ministry until his death in 1956. His successor, Lorne Sanny, said of Dawson that "some saw him as a natural leader, some as a Christian disciplinarian, others as a man of dynamic vision or great heart. Working beside him for fifteen years, I knew him primarily as a man who took God at His Word and staked all he had on His promises." Billy Graham called him "a man of vision. . . . He was always dreaming, planning, and working out new methods and means of reaching people for Christ. He seemed to have a sanctified imagination that could look beyond handicaps and circumstances and barriers. He planned big things for Christ."

"Born to Reproduce" was originally a forty-seven-minute message, given to the staff of Back to the Bible Broadcast in 1955, that burned deeply in Trotman's soul. It was later transcribed and published as a booklet that has been read by thousands over the past fifty years.

A FEW YEARS AGO, while visiting Edinburgh, Scotland, I stood on High Street just down from the castle. As I stood there, I saw a father and a mother coming toward me pushing a baby carriage. They looked very happy, were well dressed and apparently very well-to-do. I tried to catch a glimpse of the baby as they passed and, seeing my interest, they stopped to let me look at the little pink-cheeked member of their family.

I watched them for a little while as they walked on and thought how beautiful it is that God permits a man to choose one woman who seems the most beautiful and lovely to him, and she chooses him out of all the men whom she has ever known. Then they separate themselves to one another, and God in His plan gives them the means of reproduction! It is a wonderful thing that a little child should be born into their family, having some of the father's characteristics and some of the mother's, some of his looks and some of hers. Each sees in that baby a reflection of the one whom he or she loves.

Seeing that little one made me feel homesick for my own children, whom I dearly love and whose faces I had not seen for some time. As I continued to stand there, I saw another baby carriage, or perambulator as they call it over there, coming in my direction. It was a secondhand affair and very wobbly. Obviously the father and mother were poor. Both were dressed poorly and plainly, but when I indicated my interest in seeing their baby, they stopped and with the same pride as the other parents let me view their little pink-cheeked, beautiful-eyed child.

I thought as these went on their way, "God gave this little baby, whose parents are poor, everything that He gave the other. It has five little fingers on each hand, a little mouth, and two eyes. Properly cared for, those little hands may someday be the hands of an artist or a musician."

Then this other thought came to me. "Isn't it wonderful that God did not select the wealthy and the educated and say, 'You can have children,' and to the poor and the uneducated say, 'You cannot.' Everyone on earth has that privilege."

The first order ever given to man was that he "be fruitful, and multiply" (Genesis 1:22). In other words, he was to reproduce after his own kind. God did not tell Adam and Eve, our first parents, to be spiritual. They were already in His image. Sin had not yet come in. He just said, "Multiply. I want more just like you, more in My own image."

Of course, the image was marred. But Adam and Eve had children. They began to multiply. There came a time, however, when God had to destroy most of the flesh that had been born. He started over with eight people. The more than two billion people who are on earth today came from the eight who were in the ark because they were fruitful and multiplied.

Hindrances to Multiplying

Only a few things will ever keep human beings from multiplying themselves in the physical realm. If a couple is not united, they will not reproduce. This is a truth which Christians need to grasp with reference to spiritual reproduction. When a person becomes a child of God, he should realize that he is to live in union with Jesus Christ if he is going to win others to the Savior.

Another factor that can hinder reproduction is disease or impairment to some part of the body that is needed for reproductive purposes. In the spiritual realm sin is the disease that can keep one from winning the lost.

One other thing that can keep people from having children is immaturity. God in His wisdom saw to it that little children cannot have babies. A little boy must first grow to sufficient maturity to be able to earn a living, and a little girl must be old enough to care for a baby.

Everyone should be born again. That is God's desire. God never intended that man should merely live and die—be a walking corpse to be laid in the ground. The vast majority of people know that there is something beyond the grave, and so each one who is born into God's family should seek others to be born again.

A person is born again when he receives Jesus Christ. "But as many as received him, to them gave he power to become the sons of God . . . which were born, not of blood, nor of the will of the flesh, nor of the will of man, but of God" (John 1:12-13). The new birth. It is God's plan that these new babes in Christ grow. All provision is made for their growth into maturity, and then they are to multiply—not only the rich or the educated, but all alike. Every person who is born into God's family is to multiply.

In the physical realm when your children have children, you become a grandparent. Your parents are then great-grandparents, and theirs are great-great-grandparents. And so it should be in the spiritual.

Spiritual Babes

Wherever you find a Christian who is not leading men and women to Christ, something is wrong. He may still be a babe. I do not mean that he does not know a lot of doctrine and is not well-informed through hearing good preaching. I know many people who can argue the pre-, the post-, and the amillennial position and who know much about dispensations but who are still immature. Paul said of some such in Corinth, "And I, brethren, could not speak unto you as unto spiritual [or mature], but as unto carnal, even as unto babes in Christ" (1 Corinthians 3:1).

Because they were babes, they were immature, incapable of spiritual reproduction. In other words, they could not help other people to be born again. Paul continued, "I have fed you with milk, and not with meat: for hitherto ye were not able to bear it . . . ye are yet carnal [or babes]: for . . . there is among you envying, and strife, and divisions" (1 Corinthians 3:2-3). I know a lot of church members, Sunday school teachers, and members of the women's missionary society who will say to each other, "Have you heard about so-and-so?" and pass along some gossip. Such have done an abominable thing in the sight of God. How horrible it is when a Christian hears something and spreads the story! The Book says, "These six things doth the LORD hate: yea, seven are an abomination unto him: . . . a lying tongue . . ." (Proverbs 6:16-17). Oh, the Christians I know, both men and women, who let lying come in!

"He that soweth discord among brethren" (Proverbs 6:19) is

another. This is walking as a babe, and I believe that it is one of the basic reasons why some Christians do not have people born again into God's family through them. They are sick spiritually. There is something wrong. There is a spiritual disease in their lives. They are immature. There is not that union with Christ.

But when all things are right between you and the Lord, regardless of how much or how little you may know intellectually from the standpoint of the world, you can be a spiritual parent. And that, incidentally, may even be when you are very young in the Lord.

A young lady works at the telephone desk in our office in Colorado Springs. A year and a half ago, she was associated with the young communist league in Great Britain. She heard Billy Graham and accepted the Lord Jesus Christ. Soon she and a couple other girls in her art and drama school were used of the Lord to win some girls to Christ. We taught Pat and some of the others, and they in turn taught the girls whom they led to Christ. Some of these have led still other girls to Christ, and they too are training their friends. Patricia is a great-grandmother already, though she is only about a year and four months old in the Lord.

We see this all the time. I know a sailor who, when he was only four months old in the Lord, was a great-grandfather. He had led some sailors to the Lord who in turn led other sailors to the Lord, and these last led still other sailors to the Lord—yet he was only four months old.

How was this done? God used the pure channel of these

young Christians' lives in their exuberance and first love for Christ, and out of their hearts the incorruptible seed of the Word of God was sown in the hearts of other people. It took hold. Faith came by the hearing of the Word. They were born again by faith in the Lord Jesus Christ. They observed those Christians who led them to Christ and shared in the joy, the peace, and the thrill of it all. And in their joy, they wanted someone else to know.

In every Christian audience, I am sure there are men and women who have been Christians for five, ten, or twenty years but who do not know of one person who is living for Jesus Christ today because of them. I am not talking now about merely working for Christ, but about producing for Christ. Someone may say, "I gave out a hundred thousand tracts." That is good, but how many sheep did you bring in?

Some time ago I talked to twenty-nine missionary candidates. They were graduates of universities or Bible schools or seminaries. As a member of the board, I interviewed each one over a period of five days, giving each candidate from half an hour to an hour. Among the questions I asked were two that are very important. The first one had to do with their devotional life. "How is the time you spend with the Lord? Do you feel that your devotional life is what the Lord would have it to be?"

Out of this particular group of twenty-nine only one person said, "I believe my devotional life is what it ought to be." To the others my question then was, "Why is your devotional life not what it should be?"

"Well, you see, I am here at this summer institute," was a common reply. "We have a concentrated course. We do a year's work in only ten weeks. We are so busy."

I said, "All right. Let's back up to when you were in college. Did you have victory in your devotional life then?"

"Well, not exactly."

We traced back and found that never since they came to know the Savior had they had a period of victory in their devotional lives. That was one of the reasons for their sterility—lack of communion with Christ.

The other question I asked them was, "You are going out to the foreign field. You hope to be used by the Lord in winning men and women to Christ. Is that right?"

"Yes."

"You want them to go on and live the victorious life, don't you? You don't want them just to make a decision and then go back into the world, do you?"

"No."

"Then may I ask you something more? How many persons do you know by name today who were won to Christ by you and who are living for Him?" The majority had to admit that they were ready to cross an ocean and learn a foreign language, but they had not won their first soul who was going on with Jesus Christ. A number of them said that they got many people to go to church; others said they had persuaded some to go forward when the invitation was given.

I asked, "Are they living for Christ now?" Their eyes dropped.

I then continued, "How do you expect that by crossing an ocean and speaking in a foreign language with people who are suspicious of you, whose way of life is unfamiliar, you will be able to do there what you have not done here?"

These questions do not apply to missionaries and prospective missionaries only. They apply to all of God's people. Every one of His children ought to be a reproducer.

Are you producing? If not, why not? Is it because of a lack of communion with Christ, your Lord, that closeness of fellowship that is part of the great plan? Or is it some sin in your life, an unconfessed something, that has stopped the flow? Or is it that you are still a babe? "For when for the time ye ought to be teachers, ye have need that one teach you again" (Hebrews 5:12).

How to Produce Reproducers

The reason that we are not getting this gospel to the ends of the earth is not because it is not potent enough.

Twenty-three years ago, we took a born-again sailor and spent some time with him, showing him how to reproduce spiritually after his kind. It took time, lots of time. It was not a hurried, thirty-minute challenge in a church service and a hasty good-bye with an invitation to come back next week. We spent time together. We took care of his problems and taught him not only to hear God's Word and to read it, but also how to study it. We taught him how to fill the quiver of his heart with the arrows of God's Word, so that the Spirit of God could lift an arrow from his heart and place it to the bow of his lips and pierce a heart for Christ.

He found a number of boys on his ship, but none of them would go all out for the Lord. They would go to church, but when it came right down to doing something, they were "also-rans." He came to me after a month of this and said, "Dawson, I can't get any of these guys on the ship to get down to business."

I said to him, "Listen, you ask God to give you one. You can't have two until you have one. Ask God to give you a man after your own heart."

He began to pray. One day he came to me and said, "I think I've found him." Later he brought the young fellow over. Three months from the time that I started to work with him, he had found a man of like heart. This first sailor was not the kind of man you had to push and give prizes to before he would do something. He loved the Lord and was willing to pay a price to produce. He worked with this new babe in Christ, and those two fellows began to grow and spiritually reproduce. On that ship 125 men found the Savior before it was sunk at Pearl Harbor. Men off that first battleship are in four continents of the world as missionaries today. It was necessary to make a start, however. The Devil's great trick is to stop anything like this if he can before it gets started. He will stop you, too, if you let him.

There are Christians whose lives run in circles who, never-theless, have the desire to be spiritual parents. Take a typical example. You meet him in the morning as he goes to work and say to him, "Why are you going to work?"

"Well, I have to earn money."

"What are you earning money for?" you ask.

"Well," he replies, "I have to buy food."

"What do you want food for?"

"I have to eat so as to have strength to go to work and earn some more money."

"What do you want more money for?"

"I have to buy clothes so that I can be dressed to go to work and earn some more money."

"What do you want more money for?"

"I have to buy a house or pay the rent so I will have a place to rest up, so I will be fit to work and earn some more money." And so it goes. There are many Christians like that who are going in big circles. But you continue your questioning and ask, "What else do you do?"

"Oh, I find time to serve the Lord. I am preaching here and there." But down behind all of this he has the one desire to be a spiritual father. He is praying that God will give him a man to teach. It may take six months. It need not take that long, but maybe it takes him six months to get him started taking in the Word and giving it out and getting ready to teach a man himself.

So this first man at the end of six months has another man. Each man starts teaching another in the following six months. At the end of the year, there are just four of them. Perhaps each one teaches a Bible class or helps in a street meeting, but at the same time his main interest is in his man and how he is doing. So at the end of the year the four of them get together and have a prayer meeting and determine, "Now, let's not allow anything to sidetrack us. Let's give the gospel out to a lot of people, but let's check up on at least one man and see him through."

So the four of them in the next six months each get a man. That makes eight at the end of a year and a half. They all go out after another, and at the end of two years there are sixteen men. At the end of three years there are sixty-four; the sixteen have doubled twice. At the end of five years there are 1,024. At the end of fifteen and a half years there are approximately 2,147,500,000. That is the present population of the world of persons over three years of age.

But wait a minute! Suppose that after the first man, A, helps B and B is ready to get his man while A starts helping another, B is sidetracked, washes out, and does not produce his first man. Fifteen and a half years later you can cut your 2,147,500,000 down to 1,073,750,000 because the Devil caused B to be sterile.

God promised Abraham "in Isaac shall thy seed be called" (Genesis 21:12), so Abraham waited a long, long time for that son. God's promise to make Abraham the father of many nations was all wrapped up in that one son, Isaac. If Hitler had been present and had caused Isaac's death when Abraham had his knife poised over him on Mount Moriah, Hitler could have killed every Jew in that one stroke.

I believe that is why Satan puts all his efforts into getting the Christian busy, busy, busy, but not producing.

Men, where is your man? Women, where is your woman? Where is the one whom you led to Christ and who is now going on with Him?

There is a story in 1 Kings 20 about a man who gave a prisoner to a servant and instructed the servant to guard the prisoner well. But as the servant was busy here and there, the prisoner made his escape.

The curse of today is that we are too busy. I am not talking about being busy earning money to buy food. I am talking about being busy doing Christian things. We have spiritual activity with little productivity. And productivity comes as a result of what we call "follow-up."

Majoring in Reproducing

Five years ago Billy Graham came to me and said, "Daws, we would like you to help with our follow-up. I've been studying the great evangelists and great revivals, and I fail to see that there was much of a follow-up program. We need it. We are having an average of six thousand people come forward to decide for Christ in a month's campaign. I feel that with the work you have done you could come in and help us."

I said, "Billy, I can't follow up six thousand people. My work is always with individuals and small groups."

"Look, Daws," he answered, "everywhere I go I meet Navigators. I met them in school in Wheaton. They are in my school right now." (He was president of Northwestern Schools at that time.) "There must be something to this."

"I just don't have the time," I said.

He tackled me again. The third time he pled with me and said, "Daws, I am not able to sleep nights for thinking of what happens to the converts after a crusade is over."

At that time, I was on my way to Formosa (present-day Taiwan), and I said, "While I am there, I will pray about it, Billy." On the sands of a Formosan beach, I paced up and down two or three hours a day, praying, "Lord, how can I do this? I am not even getting the work done You have given me to do. How can I take six months of the year to give to Billy?" But God laid the burden upon my heart.

Why should Billy have asked me to do it? I had said to him that day before I left for Formosa, "Billy, you will have to get somebody else."

He took me by the shoulders and said, "Who else? Who is majoring in this?" I had been majoring in it.

What will it take to jar us out of our complacency and send us home to pray, "God, give me a girl or man whom I can win to Christ, or let me take one who is already won, an infant in Christ, and try to train that one so that he or she will reproduce"?

How thrilled we are to see the masses fill up the seats! But where is your man? I would rather have an "Isaac" alive than a hundred dead, sterile, or immature.

Beginning of Follow-Up

One day years ago, I was driving along in my little Model T Ford and saw a young man walking down the street. I stopped and picked him up. As he got into the car, he swore and said, "It's sure tough to get a ride." I never hear a man take my Savior's name in vain but what my heart aches. I reached into my pocket for a tract and said, "Lad, read this."

He looked up at me and said, "Haven't I seen you somewhere before?"

I looked at him closely. He looked like someone I should know. We figured out that we had met the year before on the same road. He was on his way to a golf course to caddy when I picked him up. He had gotten into my car and had started out the same way with the name "Jesus Christ." I had taken exception to his use of that name and had opened up the New Testament and shown him the way of salvation. He had accepted Jesus Christ as his Savior. In parting I had given him Philippians 1:6, "Being confident of this very thing, that he which hath begun a good work in you will perform it until the day of Jesus Christ."

"God bless you, son. Read this," I said, and sped on my merry way.

A year later, there was no more evidence of the new birth and the new creature in this boy than if he had never heard of Jesus Christ.

Winning souls was my great passion. But after I met this boy the second time on the way to the golf course, I began to go back and find some of my "converts." I want to tell you, I was sick at heart. It seemed that Philippians 1:6 was not working.

An Armenian boy came into my office one day and told

me about all the souls he had won. He said that they were all Armenians, and he had the list to prove it.

I said, "Well, what is this one doing?"

He said, "That one isn't doing so good. He is backslidden."

"What about this one?" We went all down the list and there was not one living a victorious life.

I said, "Give me your Bible." I turned to Philippians and put a cardboard right under the sixth verse, took a razor blade out of my pocket, and started to come down on the page. He grabbed my hand and asked, "What are you going to do?"

"I'm going to cut this verse out," I said. "It isn't working."

Do you know what was wrong? I had been taking the sixth verse away from its context, verses 3 through 7. Paul was not just saying, "All right, the Lord has started something. He will finish it." But you know, that is what some people tell me when they win a soul. They say, "Well, I just committed him to God."

Suppose I meet someone who has a large family and say to him, "Who is taking care of your children?"

"My family? Oh, I left them with the Lord."

Right away I would say to that one, "I have a verse for you: 'But if any provide not for his own, and specially for those of his own house, he . . . is worse than an infidel'" (1 Timothy 5:8).

Paul said to the elders of the church at Ephesus, "Take heed . . . to all the flock, over the which the Holy Ghost hath made you overseers" (Acts 20:28). You cannot make God the overseer. He makes you the overseer.

We began to work on follow-up. This emphasis on finding

and helping some of the converts went on for a couple or three years before the Navigator work started. By that time our work included fewer converts but more time spent with the converts. Soon I could say, as Paul said to the Philippians, "I thank my God upon every remembrance of you, always in every prayer of mine for you all making request with joy, for your fellowship in the gospel from the first day until now" (Philippians 1:3-5).

He followed up his converts with daily prayer and fellowship. Then he could say, "Being confident of this very thing, that he which hath begun a good work in you will perform it until the day of Jesus Christ" (Philippians 1:6). In keeping with this, the seventh verse reads: "Even as it is meet [or proper] for me to think this of you all, because I have you in my heart."

Before I had forgotten to follow up with the people God had reached through me. But from then on, I began to spend the time helping them. That is why sometime later when that first sailor came to me, I saw the value of spending three months with him. I saw an Isaac in him. Isaac had Jacob, and Jacob had the twelve, and all the rest of the nation came through them.

It Takes Time to Do God's Work

You can lead a soul to Christ in twenty minutes to a couple of hours. But it takes from twenty weeks to a couple of years to get him on the road to maturity, victorious over the sins and the recurring problems that come along. He must learn how to make right decisions. He must be warned of the various "isms" that are likely to reach out with their octopus arms and pull him in and sidetrack him.

But when you get yourself a man, you have doubled your ministry—in fact, you have more than doubled your ministry. Do you know why? When you teach your man, he sees how it is done and he imitates you.

If I were the minister of a church and had deacons or elders to pass the plate and choir members to sing, I would say, "Thank God for your help. We need you. Praise the Lord for these extra things that you do," but I would keep pressing home the big job—"Be fruitful and multiply." All these other things are incidental to the supreme task of winning a man or woman to Jesus Christ and then helping him or her to go on.

Where is your man? Where is your woman? Do you have one? You can ask God for one. Search your hearts. Ask the Lord, "Am I spiritually sterile? If I am, why am I?"

Don't let your lack of knowledge stand in the way. It used to be the plan of The Navigators in the early days that whenever the sailors were with us for supper each fellow was asked at the end of the meal to quote a verse.

I would say it this way, "Quote a verse you have learned in the past forty-eight hours if you have one. Otherwise, just give us a verse." One evening as we quoted verses around the table, my little three-year-old daughter's turn came. There was a new sailor next to her who did not think about her quoting Scripture, so without giving her an opportunity, he began. She looked up at him as much as to say, "I am a human being," then she quoted John 3:16 in her own way. "For God so loved the world, dat he gave his only forgotten son, dat *whosoever* believeth in him should not perish, but have everlasting life." She put the emphasis on the "whosoever" because when she was first taught the verse, she could not pronounce that word.

Days later that sailor came over and said to me, "You know, I was going to quote that verse of Scripture. It was the only one I knew. But I didn't really know it, not until little Ruthie quoted it. When she said 'whosoever,' I thought, 'that means me.' Back on the ship I accepted the Lord." Today that young man is a missionary in South America.

Until several years after we were married, my wife's father did not know the Lord. Here again God used children to reach a hungry heart. When Ruthie was three and Bruce was five, they went to visit Grandpa and Grandma. Grandpa tried to get them to repeat nursery rhymes. He said "Mary Had a Little Lamb" and "Little Boy Blue," but the children just looked at him and asked, "Who is Little Boy Blue?" He thought they did not know very much.

Their mother said, "They know some things. Quote Romans 3:23, Bruce." Bruce did. Then he asked, "Shall I quote another one, Grandpa?"

"Sure," said Grandpa.

Bruce began to quote verses of Scripture, some fifteen in all, and Ruth quoted some in between. This delighted Grandpa. He took them over to the neighbors and to the aunts and uncles, showing them how well these children knew the Scriptures.

In the meantime, the Word of God was doing its work. It was not long before the Holy Spirit, through the voices of babes, planted the seed in his heart. "Out of the mouth of babes and sucklings hast thou ordained strength" (Psalm 8:2).

Soul-winners are not soul-winners because of what they know, but because of the Person they know, how well they know Him, and how much they long for others to know Him.

"Oh, but I am afraid," someone says. Remember, "The fear of man bringeth a snare: but whoso putteth his trust in the LORD shall be safe" (Proverbs 29:25). Nothing under heaven except sin, immaturity, and lack of communion will put you in a position in which you cannot reproduce. Furthermore, there is not anything under heaven that can keep a newly born-again one from going on with the Lord if he has a spiritual parent to take care of him and give him the spiritual food God has provided for his normal growth.

Effects obey their causes by irresistible laws. When you sow the seed of God's Word, you will get results. Not every heart will receive the Word, but some will, and the new birth will take place. When a soul is born, give it the care that Paul gave new believers. Paul believed in follow-up work. He was a busy evangelist, but he took time for follow-up. The New Testament is largely made up of Paul's letters, which were follow-up letters to the converts.

James believed in it. "But be ye doers of the word, and not hearers only," he said in James 1:22. Peter believed in it. "As new-born babes, desire the sincere milk of the word, that ye may grow thereby" (1 Peter 2:2). John believed in it. "I have no greater joy than to hear that my children walk in truth" (3 John 4). All the writings of Peter, Paul, James, and most of John's are food for the new Christian.

The gospel spread to the known world during the first century without radio, television, or the printing press because these produced men who were reproducing. But today we have a lot of "pew-sitters"—people think that if they are faithful in church attendance, put good-sized gifts into the offering plate, and get people to come, they have done their part.

Where is your man? Where is your woman? Where is your boy? Where is your girl? Every one of us, no matter what age we are, should get busy memorizing Scripture. In one Sunday school class a woman seventy-two years of age and another who was seventy-eight finished The Navigators Topical Memory System. They then had something to give.

Load your heart with this precious Seed. You will find that God will direct you to those whom you can lead to Christ. There are many hearts ready for the gospel now.

12

THE NEED OF THE HOUR

Dawson Trotman

*"The Need of the Hour" was a message delivered
by Dawson Trotman shortly before his death.
The message was transcribed and first published in 1957.*

WHAT IS THE NEED OF THE HOUR? That depends upon the person who is thinking about it. If I'm walking along the street and see a beggar with a tin cup, what's the need of the hour? A dime. If a woman is being taken to the hospital, what's the need of the hour? A doctor.

But in Christian work, what is the need of the hour? I started to list the things that we often feel are *the* need—those things which if supplied would end our troubles.

Some say, "Well, if I just had a larger staff." Would more staff be the answer? Today many a minister would like to have an assistant, and many a mission would like to have more missionaries. The cry of returned missionaries is always for more men and women to fill up the ranks—to them, the need of the hour.

Others say, "We don't need more workers, but if we had better facilities . . . if we just had more office space and more buildings and bigger grounds and a base of operation. If we had a place like Glen Eyrie, then we could do the job."

In certain areas of the world, they say it's communications we lack or better transportation or better means to take care of health. The need of the hour on many a mission field is merely a radio. But if you get that radio, then there's another need followed by something else and something else. Many feel it is literature. I hear that in my travels all over the world, "We just lack literature."

I know of people today who are saying, "If we could just get into a certain place." For years people have been on the borders of Nepal saying, "If we could just get in." To them the need of the hour is an open door into Nepal. Right now, hundreds of people are saying, "If we could just get into China." The Bible says, "My God shall supply all your need" (Philippians 4:19). If the need were an open door into China, why doesn't God open it? "These things saith he that is holy, he that is true, he that hath the key of David, he that openeth, and no man shutteth . . . I have set before thee an open door" (Revelation 3:7-8).

Paul found closed doors, but closed doors to him weren't the problem. I believe those closed doors were used of God to show him the open doors he was to go through next. If God wanted to put His hand over the great country of China tonight, He could open the door in forty-eight hours.

Some say, "We need time. If we just had more time." Others say, "If I just weren't so old; if I were young again." People have said to me, "Daws, if I had known when I was twenty years old what I know now, I could have done a hundred times more for the Lord. Why didn't I?"

Often the biggest need of the hour seems to be money. "If we just had money—that's the answer to a larger staff, more facilities, literature, communications, and transportation. If we just had money."

What is the need of the hour? Frankly, I don't believe it is any of these. I am convinced that the God of the universe is in control, and He will supply all of these needs in His own way and in His own time, all else being right.

Let me tell you what I believe the need of the hour is. Maybe I should call it the *answer* to the need of the hour. I believe it is an army of soldiers, dedicated to Jesus Christ, who believe not only that He is God but that He can fulfill every promise He has ever made and that there isn't anything too hard for Him. It is the only way we can accomplish the thing that is on His heart—getting the gospel to every creature.

In 1948 I was in Germany for six days. I had been put in touch with Colonel Paul Maddox, chief of chaplains for all of Europe, and through his recommendation to the commanding general, I got into Germany. I invited fifty German fellows to meet with me for three days, and twenty-five of them came. I talked to them every evening for three hours, beginning to lay before them the Great Commission and the idea that I felt Germany not only needed to hear the gospel, but that Germans themselves needed to obey the Great Commission by sending missionaries.

I gave them the opportunity to ask questions during the meetings, and every once in a while, a hand would go up. I was trying to lay upon their hearts the very thing the Lord laid on the hearts of the disciples when He told them to go to every creature, make disciples of every nation, start in Jerusalem and go to the ends of the earth. One German spoke up, "But, Mr. Trotman, you don't understand. Here in Germany—some of us right in this room—don't even have an Old Testament; we only have a New Testament." But I pointed out, "When Jesus Christ gave these commandments, they didn't have even a New Testament."

Later one of them said, "But, Mr. Trotman, we have very few good evangelical books in this country. In America you have thus and so." I asked, "How many books did the disciples have?"

A little further on one of them asked, "Is it true that in America you can hear the gospel any day?" I answered, "Yes." He said, "If we had that . . . but we can't get the message out on any radio." I said, "But the disciples had never heard of a radio."

They said, "You have automobiles; we ride bicycles." I reminded them, "The disciples didn't have bicycles. Jesus rode a borrowed burro."

Now these questions didn't come up one right after the other or they would have caught on, but they were brought up during the nine hours together. Finally, one fellow spoke up and said, "In America you have money. I work twelve hours a day for sixty cents. We don't have much money." I replied, "The disciples were sent out without purse and without script."

Every excuse in the books was brought up. "We don't have

this, and we don't have that. We don't have buildings; we don't have facilities." Each time I replied, "But the twelve didn't, and He sent them out."

Then finally near the end, one fellow, a little older than the rest and with almost a bitter expression on his face, got up and said, "Mr. Trotman, you in America have never had an occupation force in your land. You don't know what it is to have soldiers of another country roaming your streets. Our souls are not our own." I responded, "The disciples lived at the time Jesus Christ lived, and their souls weren't their own. The Roman soldiers were in charge."

Then it dawned on me in a way I had never considered before. When Jesus Christ sent the eleven out, He let a situation exist which was so bad that there could never be a worse one. No printing presses, no automobiles, no radios, no television, no telephones, no buildings, not one single church, no uniforms, nothing for the vestry. He didn't even leave them a little emblem.

He left them only a job to do, but with it He said, "All power is given unto me in heaven and in earth. Go ye therefore . . ." (Matthew 28:18-19).

What does the "therefore" mean? It means, "I have the power to give you the order, and I have the power to back you to the hilt." He has *all power in heaven and earth*—not just heaven but in the earth; *all power*, not part of the power, but *all* power, which means power over the Romans and power over the communists.

Earlier Jesus Christ had said to the same little group, "Verily, verily, I say unto you, He that believeth on me . . ." He that what? ". . . *believeth* on me, the works that I do shall he do also; and greater works than these shall he do" (John 14:12).

Do you believe that statement is true? Or must you say that for a moment it makes you stop to wonder? Could it possibly be true that the Son of God would say to a human being, "The things that I do, you shall do, and greater things than these you shall do"?

I believe with all my heart that the reason so many wonderful Christians don't accomplish more in their lives is they don't believe Jesus meant what He said. They have never come to the place where they believe that the all-powerful One who commissioned them could enable them to do these greater works. The last thing He said was, "All power is given unto Me. I'm giving you all your orders now. Go and teach all nations and see that every created being hears the Word."

Now we think it is going to be a tough job even with the printing press, the radio, the airplane, and modern medicine. What do you think the early disciples thought about it? When Paul wrote to the Romans he said, "I thank my God . . . that your faith is spoken of throughout the whole world" (Romans 1:8). When he wrote to the Thessalonian church he said, "For our gospel came not unto you in word only, but also in power, and in the Holy Ghost, and in much assurance" (1 Thessalonians 1:5). And He said to the Thessalonians, who were not even as strong as the Bereans, "For from you sounded out the word of the Lord not only in Macedonia and Achaia, but also in every place your faith to God-ward is spread abroad" (1 Thessalonians 1:8).

How did the message go? Not by telephone, not by television, but by tell-a-person. That's the only method they had. It was as simple as that. Everyone was to tell someone else. "I cannot help but speak the things which I have seen and heard" was the impelling force. That's how it spread, and it did spread. They didn't need the printing press, and they didn't need materials.

Over in England they really went for Bible study and memory materials. It was hard to get them to see their value at first, but when they did, some of them felt they were a necessity. One rainy night during the Billy Graham Crusade at Wembley Stadium, around three thousand came forward at the invitation. Two clergymen came running up to me, "Mr. Trotman, Mr. Trotman, we ran out of materials! What will we do?" I said, "Relax. They probably ran out of them at Pentecost, too!" They looked at me for a minute and, obviously getting the point, said, "That's right!"

The answer is the man, not materials. Maybe the greatest problem today is that we try to put into printed form that which should go from lip to ear and heart to heart. We de-emphasize materials, and people can't understand why.

Materials are the tools. Tools by themselves are useless. If there were a young fellow beginning his study of medicine who had all the necessary instruments for a major operation, and an old doctor who just had a razor blade and a plain, ordinary crooked needle and some store string, I'd put myself into the hands of the old doctor for surgery rather than this boy over here with all his instruments, wouldn't you? It's not only the tools; it's the man who has the tools in his hands.

What is the need of the hour? I'll tell you the need of the hour. It is to believe that our God controls the universe, and when He said, "The earth shall be filled with the knowledge of the glory of the LORD, as the waters cover the sea" (Habakkuk 2:14), He meant it. That is exactly what is going to happen. The earth will be filled with the knowledge of the glory of the Lord!

Today more people than ever in a lot of our civilized countries know about Jesus Christ because of radio, literature, mission societies, Billy Graham, etc. But they only know *about* Him; they don't know Him. The Book says, "The earth shall be filled with the knowledge of the glory of the LORD, as the waters cover the sea." How much does the water cover the sea? Do you think that every square inch of sea has water in it? Yes! You have no illustration more complete than "as the waters cover the sea." That's how every tongue and tribe and nation in every single nook and corner of this earth is going to hear about Jesus Christ and His glory.

What is the need of the hour? It is to believe that "Thy God reigneth!" (Isaiah 52:7). The rain isn't coming down like you feel it should in order to have good crops. Can He send it if it's necessary? If He doesn't, can you say, "Thank you, Lord"? That's what He wants. "In every thing give thanks" (1 Thessalonians 5:18).

You don't need anything that He can't supply. Is it knowledge? Is it strength? God can do more through a weakling who is yielded and trusting than He can through a strong man who isn't. "For all the promises of God in him are yea, and in him Amen, unto the glory of God by us" (2 Corinthians 1:20).

I want the fellows and girls who come to Glen Eyrie to go away with this thought securely in their minds: "God, I'll never come to the place where I'm going to let the lack of anything persuade me that You are being hindered." I would rather you would go away with that in your hearts than with methods or materials or ideas that we may have to share with you. Because I know the potential of the man who will come to the place where he can say hour after hour, day after day, week after week, month after month, and year after year, "Lord, I believe my God reigneth."

Listen! You have an excuse if you want one. You have more than an excuse; you have hundreds of them. That isn't what's holding us back. It's that we don't live and preach the fact that He is on the throne. And when He's running the show, He will take care of all the props, even the transportation.

I was in Hong Kong on my way to India in 1948 when a Pan American flight was delayed long enough to make me miss my connection in Bangkok. I inquired if there were any way for me to get to Calcutta. The crew said, "No, not a chance in the world." Then one said, "We do have orders for this plane to go on to Calcutta, but because of regulations this crew can't take it." So I prayed, "Lord, You know about the meetings in Calcutta, and it's nothing for You to work this out."

We got to Bangkok and a radio message came: "We do not have a crew to bring this ship to Calcutta. Your crew is ordered to bring it." Only four people were on that big DC-6, and the other three didn't have to go to India for three days. I arrived in time for those meetings, and as a result, a man from Nepal came to know the Lord, a man who later became a key for getting the gospel to that closed country way up in the Himalayas.

The need of the hour, as far as I'm concerned, is to believe that God is God and that He is a lot more interested in getting this job done than you and I are. Therefore, if He is more interested in getting the job done, has all power to do it, and has commissioned us to do it, our business is to obey Him—reaching the world for Him and trusting Him to help us do it.

The Lord could easily have said to the disciples, "You fellows are only eleven men, and you lack facilities and transportation, so all I want you to do is start the fire in Jerusalem." But He didn't say that. The believers in South India testify they are glad Thomas believed Jesus Christ that he was to go to the uttermost part of the earth. I understand that the Mar Thoma Church, the largest in southern India, traces its origin back 1,900 years to the work of this disciple. Aren't you glad that Thomas didn't say to Jesus Christ, "I don't have a DC-6 yet"?

"Ye shall be witnesses unto me . . . in . . ." (Acts 1:8) not *either* Jerusalem *or* Samaria *or* Judaea or on the foreign field. You are to be witnesses, when you have the Holy Ghost, "*both* in Jerusalem, *and* in all Judaea, *and* in Samaria, *and* unto the uttermost part of the earth" (emphasis added).

Suppose you are a pastor. You have a responsibility to your people to be a shepherd to the flock. You also have a responsibility for people in other countries. You have to be concerned. The only reason you are not there telling them about Jesus Christ is because you're training the laypeople to love and serve the Lord Jesus Christ in your city, your state, and unto the uttermost part of the earth.

I close up with this, a little of the Nav story. I used to have a map of the world that I kept before me. I'd put my fingers on some of the islands—Australia, New Zealand, Okinawa, Formosa (present-day Taiwan)—and say, "Lord, let me win men for You in these places." I wasn't challenged to do this by hearing a sermon, but by a verse of Scripture, Jeremiah 33:3, "Call unto me, and I will answer thee, and shew thee great and mighty things, which thou knowest not."

In the previous chapter Jeremiah had said to the Lord, "Ah Lord GOD! behold, thou hast made the heaven and the earth by thy great power and stretched out arm, and there is nothing too hard for thee" (Jeremiah 32:17). Ten verses later the Lord says to Jeremiah, "I am the LORD, the God of all flesh: is there any thing too hard for me?" Then just a few verses later He says, "All right, if you believe me, call unto me and I will answer."

I asked a buddy, "Do you believe this verse?" He said, "Yes." I said, "I do, too, but I've never seen these great and mighty things, and I'd like to." So we started a prayer meeting every morning. We decided to meet at a certain spot, have a fire built, and be in prayer by five o'clock—not one minute after five.

We just made it a date. We prayed two hours on weekdays but met at four on Sundays to pray for our Sunday school boys by name and for the Sunday school. We prayed for Harbor City, Torrance, Long Beach, San Pedro, Los Angeles, Pasadena, and the surrounding cities from which I had received calls from young Christian fellows saying, "Come over here and show us how you're reaching these boys."

The third and fourth weeks we started to include cities up the coast—San Francisco, Oakland, Seattle, and Portland. We said, "Lord, use us in these cities." By the fourth or fifth week we had covered every state in the Union. As we listed them, we prayed, "Lord, use us to win young men to You in the state of Oregon. Use us to win young men in Massachusetts." Every morning we prayed for every one of the forty-eight states. Then about the sixth week, one of us said to the other something like this: "If we believe God is big enough to let us win men in every one of the forty-eight states, let's go all out!"

We bought a world map and left it up in the Palos Verdes hills. Each morning we'd pull this old map out and pray that the Lord would use us in China and Japan and Korea. At the end of the forty-two days, I felt a burden lift. We stopped asking God to use us and began thanking Him that He was going to do so. "Now faith is the substance of things hoped for" (Hebrews 11:1), and substance is substance. It's reality; it's something you can believe in. Faith comes by hearing, and hearing by the Word of God. We claimed the promises as we prayed. These promises were the brick, and prayer was the mortar that put them together.

After forty-two days, we discontinued our prayer meeting. Forty-eight hours later, I was in the hospital, flat on my back for a week, and I had a lot of time to think. The Minute-Men idea came, and from that, the Navigator work was born.

Three or four years later, I was rummaging around in a drawer of the living-room table when I found a little purple card—"Washington, Oregon." In another drawer was a list of names—Les Spencer from Illinois, John Dedrick of Texas, Gurney Harris from Arkansas, Ed Goodrick of Wisconsin. I discovered that men from every one of the forty-eight states had come to the Savior during those three or four years. God had answered, and these men were being trained as disciples. Then I thought of the world. "Why, Lord, am I permitted to have a part in this?" For the same reason you are.

"All power in heaven and earth is Mine. It's Mine for you to appropriate." This is not only a privilege; it's an order. He wants nothing less. God doesn't want you to take an island. He wants you to take the world. For what are you asking God? What do you want? Do you want to win a few? You'll have to start with the few, and you'll have to be successful with the few. You *can* be because Jesus said, "Follow me, and I will make you fishers of men" (Matthew 4:19). No man ever followed Jesus who didn't become a fisher of men. He never fails to do what He promised. If you're not fishing, you're not following. You have to win one before you can win five, and five before you can win five hundred. The world is before you. How big is your faith?

The need of the hour is men who want what Jesus Christ

wants and believe He wants to give them the power to do what He has asked. Nothing in the world can stop those men. Do you believe that? Do you want to be one of them? You may, but you will have to ask. "Call unto me, and I will answer thee, and shew thee great and mighty things, which thou knowest not." Years ago, when I prayed for Formosa, I couldn't have comprehended what I'm seeing now. But that's the way He has promised it will be; so when you call, ask big!

NOTES

CHAPTER 3: CLAIMING THE PROMISE

1. John R. W. Stott, "The Living God Is a Missionary God," in *You Can Tell the World*, ed. James Berney (Downers Grove, IL: InterVarsity Press, 1979), 20.

2. Ibid., 16.

3. Dr. Ralph Winter, letter to author, July 18, 1990.

4. Bible Hub, "Commentaries: Genesis 17:5," accessed December 1, 2020, https://biblehub.com/commentaries/genesis/17-5.htm.

5. R. A. Torrey, *How to Pray* (Old Tappan, NJ: Spire Books, Fleming H. Revell Co., 1970), 41.

6. According to the U.S. Bureau of Census, in 2007 (when this essay was written), 56.6 percent of the 6.6 billion people in the world lived in Asia.

7. India is home to 1.1 billion people as of 2007.

8. "Mission Frontiers," *Bulletin of the U.S. Center for World Mission*, vol. 12, nos. 1 and 2 (Pasadena, CA: January–February 1990), 19, http://www.missionfrontiers.org/issue/article/catch-the-vision-of-your-part-in-the-big-picture.

9. As of 2007, when this essay was written, conservative estimates indicate there are upward of 60 million Christians in China.

10. Ralph Winter and David A. Fraser, "World Mission Survey," in *Perspectives on the World Christian Movement* (Pasadena, CA: William Carey Library, Institute of International Studies, 1981), 344. In 2007, there were an estimated 380 million Christians in Africa.

11. S. D. Gordon, *What It Will Take to Change the World* (Grand Rapids, MI: Baker Book House, 1981), 112; and *Quiet Talks on Prayer* (Old Tappan, NJ: Fleming H. Revell Co., 1903), 15, 82.

12. Warren and Ruth Myers, *PRAY: How to Be Effective in Prayer* (Colorado Springs, CO: NavPress, 1983), 143.

13. Edward Judson, *The Life of Adoniram Judson* (New York: Randolph & Co., 1883).

CHAPTER 7: WORK: WHERE LIFE AND CALLING MEET

1. Mark Greene, *The Great Divide* (London: London Institute for Contemporary Christianity, 2010).

2. Studs Terkel, *Working: People Talk About What They Do All Day and How They Feel About What They Do* (New York: The New Press, 2004), Introduction.

3. Jerry and Mary White, *On the Job: Survival or Satisfaction* (Colorado Springs: NavPress, 1989).

4. Consider using the *Scriptural Roots of Commerce*, by Global Commerce Network, at www.globalcommercenetwork.com.

CHAPTER 9: READING THE BIBLE WITH FRIENDS WHO DON'T BELIEVE IT

1. See Matthew 13:1-23, 36-43 (the parable of the sower); 13:24-30 (the parable of the weeds); 20:1-16 (the parable of the workers in the vineyard); Mark 4:26-29 (the parable of the growing seed); John 15:1-17 (the illustration of the vine and the branches).

2. *Scriptural Roots of Commerce*, available at www.globalcommercenetwork .com.

CHAPTER 10: HOW DO WE CREATE A LIFE-GIVING ATMOSPHERE?

1. Amy Martin, senior director of culture and engagement at Highpoint Church in Naperville, Illinois. Used with permission.

THE NAVIGATORS® STORY

THANK YOU for picking up this NavPress book! We hope it has been a blessing to you.

NavPress is a ministry of The Navigators. The Navigators began in the 1930s, when a young California lumberyard worker named Dawson Trotman was impacted by basic discipleship principles and felt called to teach those principles to others. He saw this mission as an echo of 2 Timothy 2:2: "And the things you have heard me say in the presence of many witnesses entrust to reliable people who will also be qualified to teach others" (NIV).

In 1933, Trotman and his friends began discipling members of the US Navy. By the end of World War II, thousands of men on ships and bases around the world were learning the principles of spiritual multiplication by the intentional, person-to-person teaching of God's Word.

After World War II, The Navigators expanded its relational ministry to include college campuses; local churches; the Glen Eyrie Conference Center and Eagle Lake Camps in Colorado Springs, Colorado; and neighborhood and citywide initiatives across the country and around the world.

Today, with more than 2,600 US staff members—and local ministries in more than 100 countries—The Navigators continues the transformational process of making disciples who make more disciples, advancing the Kingdom of God in a world that desperately needs the hope and salvation of Jesus Christ and the encouragement to grow deeper in relationship with Him.

NAVPRESS was created in 1975 to advance the calling of The Navigators by bringing biblically rooted and culturally relevant products to people who want to know and love Christ more deeply. In January 2014, NavPress entered an alliance with Tyndale House Publishers to strengthen and better position our rich content for the future. Through *THE MESSAGE* Bible and other resources, NavPress seeks to bring positive spiritual movement to people's lives.

If you're interested in learning more or becoming involved with The Navigators, go to navigators.org. For more discipleship content from The Navigators and NavPress authors, visit thedisciplemaker.org. May God bless you in your walk with Him!

navpress.com

CP1308